Real Christians ~~Don't~~ Dance!

Real Christians ~~Don't~~ Dance!

JOHN FISCHER

BETHANY HOUSE PUBLISHERS
MINNEAPOLIS, MINNESOTA 55438
A Division of Bethany Fellowship, Inc.

Published by Bethany House Publishers
A Division of Bethany Fellowship, Inc.
6820 Auto Club Road, Minneapolis, Minnesota 55438

Printed in the United States of America

Library of Congress Cataloging-in-Publication Data

Fischer, John.
    Real Christians don't dance / John Fischer.

    p. cm.
    1. Evangelicalism—United States—Controversial literature.
2. Christian life—1960–   I. Title.
BR1642.U5f54   1988   248.4—dc19   88-458
ISBN 1-556-61010-6   CIP

To Ruth Martin,

*whose unrelenting demand for truth
has pulled me both in to what I believe
and out of what I don't.*

ACKNOWLEDGMENTS

The writing in this book spans a six-year period and some of the insights go back to the early seventies. I would like to gratefully acknowledge the staff and elders of Peninsula Bible Church, Palo Alto, California, whose faithful teaching and life-style shaped the beginning of many of those thoughts. I want to thank John Styll and *CCM* magazine for providing, through a regular column, an opportunity to develop as a writer, and an obligation to discover, once a month, where God was working—and not working—in my life. Thanks also to Dan and Kathy Cunningham and their children who have always seen me as an artist, even when I couldn't. And special thanks to Kathy whose unselfish discernment and brilliant literary criticism were always only a phone call away. And finally, I want to thank my wife, Marti, for all the times she made me frustrated by forcing me to face what I knew was not my best.

FOREWORD

by Tony Campolo

Sacred cows make great hamburgers. John Fischer understands that and in this book does a job on some of the sacred cows that have been idols for many of us—those cultural idiosyncracies which often hinder our growth and development as Christians. He wants us to escape from a host of trivial pursuits which often absorb our attention and energies so that we have little to give to the weightier concerns of the Christian faith.

In this book, John lets us know that he believes much goes on in the name of religion which focuses on petty pieties while ignoring the biblical urgency "to love justice, do mercy and walk humbly" with one's brothers and sisters. In an effort to get us out of such a bind, he takes us on a trip through a variety of personal experiences in which he struggled to rid his faith of cultural accretions. In each vignette about his life, he provides us with graphic evidence of how a person growing up in the context of an evangelical church and a good Christian family might have to struggle and even be somewhat deviant in order to have a faith that makes sense and has the marks of personal ownership.

I can identify with John's struggles because in many ways they have been my own. When I became a Christian, the leaders of my church told me that "the world" would try to destroy my commitment to Christ by pressuring me to conform to its sinful ways. What I found was just the opposite. The kids at my high school put very little pressure on me to conform. At our school there was a general consensus that everybody was entitled to do his or her own thing. As a matter of fact, my newly acquired religiosity was heralded as "far out" and interestingly strange. But while the kids at the high school made few demands of me, the people at church were not so liberating. The church folk had clearly delineated expectations for me, and they quickly

7

taught me what I could and could not do. It was the stifling effect of these expectations of the religious that almost destroyed my faith. It was the pressure of church people rather than the seduction of the world that almost did me in.

John Fischer understands people like me, and if you are like me, you will like this book and be helped by it. The ways in which Fischer worked through the confinements of religiosity into the freedom of spirituality are useful examples for all of us who are caught up in similar treks.

Jesus taught that the constraints of religiously legitimated cultural legalism had to be challenged. In this book, Fischer tries to follow in the footsteps of His master and strike out against those same kinds of biblically ungrounded ideas which smother the joyful freedom that can be had in Jesus. When you finish this book, you probably will get a better feel for that freedom and it may be that the next time someone asks you, "Can Christians dance?", you will answer, "Some can . . . and some can't." John would love your answer.

PREFACE

by Leighton Ford

John Fischer thinks and probes and this is evident in his writing. He is seeking to uncover "Christlike" thinking, not just "contemporary Christian" thinking.

These writings, I believe, will prove both entertaining and provocative for those who want to examine the routine of life in a creative way.

CONTENTS

*We played the flute for you,
and you did not dance.*

—Jesus Christ

REAL CHRISTIANS DON'T DANCE?

*S*o is this it? This is what it comes down to: *real Christians don't dance*? Moses parted the water for this? Rahab tucked the spies away in her closet for this? Jael drove a tent peg into the head of Sisera for this? Jesus died and rose again, martyrs were sawn in two, and the Church has prevailed for almost two thousand years against the gates of hell so that Christians today can live out this ever important testimony to the waiting, watching world: *real Christians don't dance*?

Well, it's time to get a few things straight. The world isn't waiting for Christians; the world doesn't care. In fact, no one but Christians care about what Christians do or don't do. The world is not watching Christians except to be entertained by the latest episode of spicy details in the rise and fall of TV Evanjel-lorama. What we have is clearly an in-house problem.

When I carried notes to school from my parents each week excusing me from social dancing in the fifth grade, no one really cared except my parents—who cared a whole lot. They likened my testimonial stand to Daniel's before Nebuchadnezzar. I cared, too, feeling alone and abnormal, standing to the side while everyone else had a good time. My friends simply never understood. I didn't either; it was just something I wasn't supposed to do, something that made me different from everybody else.

Why have Christians made such important issues out of non-issues? I think it's because we want something clearly identifiable that will distinguish us from the world. We want to be different. We want being born again to evidence itself in some clear, tangible way in our world.

This much is good, but godly men and women have historically distinguished themselves in much more important ways than staying off the dance floor. Modern Christianity has gravitated to a list of *do*'s and *don't*s because this spells out the distinctiveness so clearly. Being born again becomes a simple matter of following a prescribed formula.

Not that there aren't any *do*'s and *don't*s in the Christian faith. The New Testament is full of directives for godly behavior. But the biblical guidelines are much different than the ones found in popular Christianity, and it doesn't take a genius to figure out the difference. The rules for behavior in the Bible deal with less noticeable things, and involve commands which are harder to fulfill than the non-issues we have created for our own Christian identity.

Which is easier to follow: *real Christians don't envy* or *real Christians don't dance*? Which one gets noticed first: *real Christians don't lust* or *real Christians don't smoke*? Which is harder to comply with: *real Christians love their enemies* or *real Christians go to church on Sundays*?

Looking at it this way, it soon becomes evident that we are creating our own manageable system of weighing and measuring ourselves. We are not unlike the Pharisees, who regulated righteousness into a long, involved list of steps and procedures, cumbersome indeed, but fulfillable.

We're really touching the age-old problem of the *good* as the enemy of the *best*. As soon as the Christian life becomes self-attainable, it ceases to require faith and loses its seasoning of humility and grace. We've exchanged a far more involved and demanding set of directives for a simpler, more obvious package. We've exchanged the Bible for a seminar notebook, the Gospel for a tract, the church for a television show.

Yes, I'm afraid it has come down to this: *real Christians don't dance*. Don't you think Moses parted the water for something more?

Dressing up,
Lookin' good and feelin'
so alive.
Dressing up,
Got the clothes and
I'm goin' in style.

—Barbie and the Rockers

PART

DRESSING UP

$\mathcal{I}$ would like to go dancing all dressed up, but I'm not sure what to wear. You see, I haven't been dancing much; it's been against my religion most of my growing-up days—or at least I thought it was. Things are changing now, but it's hard to break away from those old taboos.

What do we wear for the dance of life? David danced before the Ark of the Covenant in front of all Israel, but I'm not sure I want to wear what he wore—or more accurately: didn't wear! Do clothes mask or express who we are? Do we dress to hide, to blend in, or to stand out? Is appearance really everything?

We live in a culture that tells us that image is everything. Our world strives for proper appearances. The successful company is not necessarily the one with the best product but the one with the best image. The most beautiful girl is the one who best resembles the model on the cover of the magazine. The best rock group is the one with the most outrageous stage show, costuming, and marketing hype.

In the midst of a dress-for-success world, how do we find out what is real? What actually lies behind the images? Is the product this company markets actually a good one? Is the real life of a beautiful model everything it's made out to be? Can this rock-and-roll band, decked out for the stage, really play music?

In his victory romp celebrating the return of the Ark of the Covenant, David took a rather shocking approach to portraying his kingship. His wife Michal, who had been watching from her bedroom window, sarcastically derided him: "How the king of Israel has distinguished himself today, disrobing in the sight of the slave girls of his servants as any vulgar fellow would!" He replied, "It was before the Lord, who chose me rather than your father [Saul] or anyone from his house when he appointed me ruler over the Lord's people Israel—I will celebrate before the Lord. I will become even more undignified than this, and I will be humiliated in my own eyes. But by these slave girls you spoke of, I will be held in honor" (2 Sam. 6:20–22).

It appears, at least in David's case, that there must be a dressing down before dressing up is appropriate. David was a king by calling, not by pedigree. He was a shepherd boy whose only filigree was faith. His royal clothes carried no significance before God, so he took them off to dance. It was truly a dance of grace.

I, on the other hand, have come to accept many aspects of my Christianity as an inheritance from a Christian culture. I have worn robes from youth that I now realize must come off if I am ever to dance the dance of life. I will probably be considered undignified by the Michals in the windows and held in honor by the slaves of the servants.

If that's the case, then so be it; but get this stuff off me . . . I want to dance!

DESIGNER CHRISTIANITY

I'm ready to go dancing, but what do I wear?
The clothes the Church gave me are totally square.
I need to hit the floor with a little flare—
Something that looks like I'm going somewhere.
So dress me up in the clothes of my culture.
Give me some style; put on the luster.
And they'll think that the Gospel has got to be keen
When they see me dressed up in my Calvin Klein jeans!

A good picture says it all; and this one was good. When Calvin Klein first came out with topless designer-jean ads, one artist gave us a backside view of a female clad only in jeans. On the back pocket, a partially torn-away patch bearing the familiar fish sign with the letters *JESUS* covered all but the first four letters of "Calvin Klein." The illustration was entitled "Dressing Up the Gospel."

That picture perfectly captured a Christianity in confusion. The Jesus sticker was reminiscent of the sixties, but not the jeans. Sixties' jeans had holes, and the tacky Jesus patch would have been found amid various other patches, macrame, and graffiti. Those were the days when faith was real and radical. A generation of hippies had temporarily rejected the materialism of their parents and found, to their surprise, that the words of Jesus were also seasoned with anti-establishment salt.

The old jeans were folded away in the attic, materialism was embraced with greater intensity than the former generation had ever imagined, and the Gospel was joined to Calvin Klein. And in many ways this unlikely marriage appears as incompatible as the sign of the fish over tight-fitting designer jeans.

In essence, the new born-again society that emerged from the revivals of the sixties has dressed itself up in the clothes of popular culture.

In the process, it has also tried to dress up the Gospel by making it easy, fun, and popular. It has produced a Gospel compatible with materialism, shaping it to feel good, sensational, and glamorous. In short, it has dressed up the Gospel in whatever designer clothes the world happens to be admiring.

It may be an innocent mistake born from sincere evangelistic fervor, but in the end, fashion robs the Gospel of its power. The new born-again society has accepted the misguided assumption that it must convince the world that being a Christian is a good thing. But not only that, becoming born again is the thing to do. It's hip.

In light of this, we need to pay close attention to Paul's words in 2 Corinthians: "Therefore, since through God's mercy we have this ministry, we do not lose heart. Rather, we have renounced secret and shameful ways; we do not use deception, nor do we distort the word of God. On the contrary, by setting forth the truth plainly we commend ourselves to every man's conscience in the sight of God" (2 Cor. 4:1–2).

The Apostle is telling us that the Gospel doesn't need to be tampered with or altered in any way. There's nothing to hide, nothing to change. The Gospel is perfectly capable of taking care of itself; our only responsibility is to proclaim it *plainly* before every man's conscience.

Each person, deep in their own conscience, will ultimately accept or reject the message of salvation through Jesus Christ. The choice someone makes is beyond our control. Our business is to clearly present the truth, not by dressing up the Gospel, but by living out the reality of our lives before people. Paul put it simply: "We commend ourselves."

Nothing needs to be done *to* the Gospel. Everything's already been done. But there is much that needs to be done in our lives *by* the Gospel. There is hope to be expressed, sin to be confessed, forgiveness to be embraced, suffering to be endured, glory to be shared, love to be received, and love to be given. It is the presence of all this happening in our lives that we commend to someone else.

If the Gospel is alive in me and I introduce myself to someone, I am introducing them to the Gospel. If it is not alive in me, no amount of dressing it up is going to convince anyone; but, on the contrary, it will mask the real truth.

The issue, therefore, is not how to present the Gospel, but how to make certain it is living in me—a much more difficult issue. It means deep questioning, soul-searching, and observing myself continually in light of the truth. "Undressing" would be a more appropriate expression of this process than "dressing up."

So David was right after all. Dressing up, if it protects us from having to be honest, is nothing more than cover-up. The success of the Gospel in our present age does not depend on how attractively it is packaged, but on how honestly real Christians are living out their lives in the world. That's a message you simply cannot dress up, especially if you tell the whole truth about yourself.

We don't use deception. We won't draw people into a net and then surprise them with the Gospel. We set forth the Gospel plainly through words of truth and words of honesty from our lives. We trust God, the Great Designer, to handle His own image.

THE GLITTER AND THE GLORY

*H*ardly any other aspect of Christianity is more affected by the proliferation of popular appearances and images than our concept of glory. *Glory* used to be strictly a spiritual term, associated with the radiance of the character and presence of God and His heaven. Old Testament revelations of the glory of God sent prophets, as well as holy men and women, scurrying for cover.

Today, glory is more commonly associated with popularity and fame. Stars that shine in our culture are found on small fluorescent screens in gloomy living rooms, not outside in the expanse of the night sky. Our heroes are bigger than life, bolstered by special effects, resilient stunt people, and perfect camera angles.

The presence of television in every home makes it possible for millions to focus on only a few. This media attention, though powerful in its ability to homogenize widely held cultural values, is a far cry from displaying any idea of real glory; instead, it is mere glitter. It is a fabrication of the human image and we all, whether we realize it or not, fall down and worship in one way or another.

Popular Christianity has bought into the glitter. Indeed, it is largely the media that has made Christianity popular. Twenty-five years ago it was not popular to be a Christian. Now, being born again could get a person elected to public office. Christian TV, Christian music, Christian political coalitions, and a conservative wave of public opinion have all converged to bring this about. Whether it's good or bad, Christians are getting more publicity today.

But is this always the kind of publicity we want? Can glitter be used to advance the kingdom of God? When we broadcast our story, is it real, or is it just as fabricated as the soap opera on the next channel? The power of TV is also its greatest temptation: the power to create an imaginary reality that becomes the shared experience of millions. The temptation is to make that reality more then real, more what we want it to be than what it is. Christians have succumbed to this temptation as much as anyone—maybe more.

Therefore, the task at hand is to learn how not to confuse our culture's glitter with real glory. This is no easy task, but gaining an understanding of what real glory is would be a good beginning. The Apostle Paul carefully delineated differences in glory that surprisingly foreshadow the same confusion we experience between glitter and glory: "Now if the ministry that brought death, which was engraved in letters on stone [the Law], came with glory, so that the Israelites could not look steadily at the face of Moses because of its glory, fading though it was, will not the ministry of the Spirit be even more glorious?" (2 Cor. 3:7, 8).

He is speaking of two different ministries and the corresponding glory attached to each. The first thing to notice is that Paul is comparing ministries. His distinction is subtle, not between good guys and bad guys, but between good guys and good guys. Moses was certainly a man of God seeking to do the best he could, but the glory attached to his activity somehow falls short of what the Spirit has planned for us.

Upon more careful examination, Moses' glory typifies the glitter of our present culture. Moses exemplifies the Law and all that the Law embraces: perfection, self-effort, and performance.

25

The Law leads to frustration and guilt, and always ends in death; because the Law is perfect, no one can fully obey it. But the Spirit brings us grace, forgiveness, power, and adequacy for the very life we are required to live.

When we look at it this way, the path of obedience to the Law, with such a depressing array of qualities, appears to have no chance at all. But it does because it still has a glory attached to it. It's the same glitter that fools people today.

Let's face it, the glory of Moses' face must have been quite impressive. He could have given Michael Jackson a real run for his money even without a television camera, a light show, or a glittering glove! In fact, his face was so bright that people couldn't even look steadily at it, just as we can't stare at the sun for any length of time without damaging our eyes.

This kind of glory easily fools us. How quickly we attribute a radiant personality or great charisma to the presence of God. But in Moses' case it wasn't the *present* presence of God; it was the *past* presence: leftover glory. And because it was leftover, Paul said it was fading.

This kind of glory always starts big and then fizzles. It begins with God but ends with us. The brilliance of Moses' face was real glory from being with the real God, but it faded because he had to leave God on the mountain and trust in human sufficiency, his own and Israel's, to keep it going.

How often do we start with big plans, only to leave God on the mountain? Even the greatest vision from God can fade when we take our trust from Him and focus it in ourselves: our own talent, our own personality, or our own experience.

Paul says there is a glory more glorious than this fading glitter. It eclipses the brightness of Moses' face or the glory of any magazine-cover face. It's a glory that comes from the ministry of the Spirit in us. The Spirit knows we are destined to shine brighter than the sun in our glorified bodies, so He is in no hurry to put on a light show now. He is content to operate on the quiet level of changing our lives. He has a long-term commitment to working the character of God into our lives on a daily basis.

Glory on a human level starts big and fades like the face of Moses. It relies heavily on images of success that can be fabricated and sold in a media-oriented world. But the glory of the Spirit starts small, hardly noticeable, and grows steadily from one degree of glory to another. Day by day we become more like Him.

The Spirit's glory is not activated by a spotlight. People with the confidence of the Spirit in their lives can walk with ease in all situations, knowing that the glory of God will always be seen in them, sometimes even in spite of them.

This glory does not come and go on demand. It's either there or not there. We have either the fading glitter of our own human effort or the increasing glory of the character of God being built into our lives.

All that glitters is not gold.

GOD ON TRIAL

*T*here is a major problem that confronts popularized ministry in America today: *How do we convince the world that Christianity is true?* We tend to take the witness stand and try to prove the truth of the Gospel by our experience. It is a sad state of affairs, however, when God has to stand trial, waiting to see if our testimony is going to over-power the testimony of the world. At best, I fear He's headed for a hung jury.

I have been at *est* meetings in which the testimonies of changed lives and the enthusiastic support of others have run circles around any Christian testimony meeting I have ever at-tended. The Mormon family commitment and the evangelical fervor of the Jehovah's Witnesses put us to shame. There is more love and compassion expressed on one Jerry Lewis telethon than there is in a whole year of Sunday morning services in our av-erage Christian church. Pagan Africans speak in tongues and Christian Scientists are healed. And let's face it, Johnny Carson is certainly more entertaining than most of today's Christian talk-show hosts.

So what?

If the historical death and resurrection of Jesus Christ is not enough proof, then all the experiences of all the Christians who have ever lived will not prove anything either. The core of our message must not be our experience; it must be the truth. Satan can imitate (and often outshine) any Christian experience, but he is helpless against the truth of the Gospel: the death and resurrection of Jesus Christ.

If we can understand this, we will be set free from the unnecessary theological defenses we use to confront the world. Let's look at a few of the usual defenses:

Defense No. 1

Christians have more fun.

I don't find the evidence for this in the Scriptures, unless you call being rejected, beaten, thrown in jail, sawn in two, or hung on a cross *fun*. Exciting maybe, but certainly not fun. Let's face it, the pleasures of the world are fun—momentary, for sure, but fun. A Christian's job is not to compete with the pleasures of the world but to get on with living out the Gospel.

Defense No. 2

Non-Christians are all miserable degenerates.

Either they are helplessly trapped by the lure of sin or they are aggressively pursuing (and thoroughly enjoying) a malicious way of life, out to make as many recruits as possible on their highway to hell. What happens when we find non-Christians who are disciplined, moral, generous, kind, and relatively happy? We immediately begin to hunt for that fatal flaw in their character which will prove that they really have been miserable, Christless wretches, and even their apparently good deeds have sprung from an evil source.

Instead, we must realize every man and woman bears the image of God and as such is capable of producing some goodness on this planet. Christians must learn to appreciate the dignity of man regardless of salvation. Worth is not the *result* of salvation, it is the *reason* for it, and the reason hell is such a tragedy.

Until we realize that we have something to learn from every

human being who walks the face of this earth, and that our humanity lies in even the most despicable of sinners, we will never be able to present the untainted, simple truth of the Gospel that will set us *all* free.

Defense No. 3

Donna Summer's testimony carries more weight than my mother's.

My mother, along with countless others like her, spends hours in her closet praying people into the kingdom. But we never showcase her or any of the rest of these intercessors. Instead, we constantly parade the sensational, the attractive, trying to draw the attention of the world and convince them that Christ is real. But in doing so, aren't we baiting the hook with the very enticements from which Jesus wants to set us free?

Defense No. 4

Christians don't fall into "big" sins. Unfortunately, we're getting over this one the hard way: by having the dirty laundry dragged out and hung in the street. The sad part is we should have done this ourselves. It's called confession. But it is hard to agree that sin is in your life when you're trying to prove you're a Christian by how much better you are for being one.

Christians must realize that sin is not the problem. Sin was taken care of 2,000 years ago on the cross. The problem with Christians is getting up enough courage and belief in that cross to confess the sin and enough humility to accept the forgiveness that is offered. That's hard to do when you have so much to prove.

The answer to all this is really very simple: We don't have to prove a thing by our experience, or by anything else for that matter. God has already stood trial, been sentenced, and put to death—never to be put on trial again. His resurrection is the final proof.

YOUNG MAN, OLD MAN, SOUP SPOON

— ACT ONE —

*T*he two men walked down the street in the direction of the coffee shop. The old man was somewhere in his eighties and had been walking with the Lord longer than the younger one had been alive. Actually, "walking" is too passive a word . . . more like "fighting." He was a feisty old man and his fight had been one for truth and honesty from himself and from God. The resulting wisdom and lively charm made his younger companion look forward to these meetings.

As the two men approached the coffee shop, they happened to pass a young woman. She was dressed in such a way as to take fullest advantage of the warm weather and her physical attributes. The awkward silence that followed in her wake confused the young man. He had known this silence before with his peers. It was always full of uncomfortable questions like "Do I ignore this? Do I break the tension by making a joke? Do I say something spiritual?" With his peers, he could understand it, but with an old man whose eyesight was dim and whose glands were most likely dried up, it didn't make sense. His curiosity finally got the best of him and he blurted out, "Do you ever get over that?"

"Not yet," replied the old man with a twinkle. The young man was shocked. At his age, his maturity, his wisdom—and he was still dealing with lust? Moments later, seated in the coffee shop, the young man pursued the conversation. "Do you mean to tell me that it doesn't get any better?"

The old man's appearance was a fitting backdrop for his forthcoming reply. The skin on his face hung low on the bones, pulled down by eighty years of gravity. Small, stubby gray hairs grew out of brown moles on his cheeks, and who knows what was growing out of his ears. His coat hung low like the skin of his face, and nothing—the coat, the shirt, the pants, or the tie— matched. His tie was the unwary target of much gesturing with a half-filled soup spoon.

He leaned into the table and smiled over the rim of his glasses. "Do I look like it's getting any better?" Another blotch of soup decorated his tie.

The young man laughed at the comical scene across the table, but his mind was whirling with the implications of the old man's point of view. He had always assumed the older one got, the easier it was to be godly.

"Well, you dirty old man!" he joked.

"No, no. Healthy old buzzard maybe, but not dirty old man."

"What's so healthy about lust?"

"Nothing," said the old man. "But who said anything about lust? What's so *unhealthy* about sexuality?"

The young man plunged into his soup du jour with greater vigor. That point had hit close to home. It made him wonder how much of his own sexuality he was denying in his struggle with sin.

"But it's hard to affirm your sexuality when you're fighting lust all the time," he thought out loud.

"That's exactly your problem," said the old man. "You're expending too much energy fighting lust when you've got much better things to do with your sexuality."

"Name one."

The old man's voice was more deliberate than before. "Our society is so obsessed with the physical expression of sexuality that the emotional and spiritual aspects are overlooked. Sexuality is a vital part of your God-given humanity. It's not just an isolated physical act. You can turn your sexual power outward to serve and care for others rather than keeping it to yourself in a closet."

The old man's soup spoon now doubled as both a band director's baton and a sword jabbing his point at the young man across the table. Its original function had long been usurped.

"What I'm really trying to get at is that it's okay to be a human being—a human sexual being. God made man male and female and He said it was good." The soup spoon baton crescendoed to its final note. "And after eighty years of living it out, I can say it's good too.

"Of course, there's another solution to the problem," he said after a brief pause.

"What's that?"

"You could become a eunuch. You know, most Christian men think that's what Jesus meant when He said, '. . . if it offends you, cut it off!' "

At that statement the young man spewed a mouthful of water over the table. Between coughs and sputters, he said, "No thanks!"

The old man leaned forward for the last time, sword in hand. "Excuse me," he said, "but that's how you've been dealing with this matter so far."

The two men sat frozen in each other's stare for an instant until the younger one broke the silence. "I . . . I think you spilled some soup on your tie."

"Oh, so I did," said the old man, leaning back, lifting up his glasses so he could see under his nose. "Oh, well . . . kind of blends in with the overall design, doesn't it?"

OF PEELINGS AND PEDESTALS

I grew up under the watch-ful eye of a mainline evangelical denomination. Every Sunday I attended Sunday School in the morning and Christian Endeavor at night. Once a month I stayed late for a Sunday-night sing after church. I remember the sings because there was always a trumpet trio playing a double-tongued version of "Wonderful Grace of Jesus." The best ones could triple-tongue the last verse.

I remember a diagram someone once chalked on a church blackboard that divided my life up like a pie. The spiritual pieces included going to church, reading my Bible, praying, and wit-nessing. I did all those, and then I went on to a Christian college. I kept all the pieces in place.

I have always been an insider at church, a perpetual "after" in terms of the "before" and "after" of being a Christian. I have always worn a white hat. I'm the guy all the mothers in church referred to when they nagged their sons, "Why don't you be like him?"

I wasn't very popular with my friends.

Once I wrote the following poem:

34

I hate it here
Up on this pedestal.
How did I get here anyway?
Did someone put me here
Or did I climb up
All by myself?
Never mind how I got here—
I just want to get off.
I hate it here
Up on this pedestal.
I know what I'll do . . .
I'll jump!
And when everything is splattered on the floor,
Then whatever stands
Will have to stand on its own,
And whatever rises
Will have to be real.

I'd like to think that I've jumped, but I'm not so sure I ever have. It's hard to tell, because I've learned to act out the acceptable Christian life so well. If I have really jumped, I think I've crawled back up more times than I realize.

As a result of this familiarity with Christian society, my salvation story has not been so much about conversion as it has been about extraction, like peeling away the outer layer of traditional Christian expectations from the orange of my Christian experience, trying to determine what to keep and what to throw away.

It's not a simple process at all, not a succulent ball with a thin, white skin separating easily from its curling peel. No, real emotional response to God has had to be wrung from a thousand stirring musical chords, real obedience pried from layers of traditional Christian expectations. Heart has had to be shaken out of assumption, love distilled from law.

A question arises as I tear at the incorrigible fusion of fruit and peel. While sticky juice squirts in my face and rolls down my wrist, I discover part of the flesh adhering to the peel, pulling away from the meat of the orange. I wonder, *How do I keep from throwing away good pieces of fruit along with the peeling?*

It's a battle not to fall into cynicism at this point. It's inevitable that I will at some point tear away good fruit. If I openly discuss this process, I may hurt someone by condemning some good thing that has been born in myself or someone else. I have decided I must take this risk.

I used to think it was only necessary to speak the truth and let it go at that. If people misinterpreted it, that was not my problem. But I think differently now. The role of the prophet is to stand before truth and cause it to shine in relationship to current situations. Part of that illumination process is to reinterpret what has been misinterpreted. The Old Testament prophets and Jesus all did this.

There is too much in America that labels itself Christian; it cannot all be true. The difficult thing about being a Christian today is that it has become too easy. I can't help but think that some folks are coming along merely for the ride. But so what if they are? I cannot judge them. My responsibility is to reinterpret the message for myself and be honest about this personal interrogation. So I peel away at this orange, not because I want to destroy anyone, but because I want, with all my heart, to get at the truth.

It would be easy to say, "I'm a Christian today because my good parents taught me the Word of God from childhood, because I spent all those hours in church, because I enjoyed a consistent family altar, because so many Christians around me provided fine examples, etc." All of these things are noble, all valuable in their own right. But in fact, I'm a Christian today because God has chosen to have a relationship with me, and I, in turn, have chosen to have one with Him.

To return to such an elementary understanding—what would be natural baby steps for a new convert from outside the conclaves of the Christian subculture—has been (and continues to be) like peeling this orange. The more I work at it, the more I discover it is a very thick-skinned orange, the kind that makes me wonder, as I stare at the pile of orange-and-white chunks in the sink and then at the squishy pulp in my hand—was there more peel here than orange? More Christianity than Christ? More fundamentalism than faith? More law than love? And if there was, how much is still there?

36

MAGICAL MINISTRY TOUR

*N*o word is more misused and misinterpreted in popular Christianity than *ministry*. It is the reason for everything: the justification for a top ten hit and the toleration of substandard performance. It legitimizes one person's right to accumulate and hoard money while it supports another's right to beg for it. It serves simultaneously as an excuse to work or not to work. The word *ministry* covers so much ground that it no longer carries any significant impact. Instead, it leaves nebulous impressions and feelings.

The popular understanding of ministering to people is to touch them in some spiritual sense. But in what way—what does it mean for someone to be blessed? Was it an emotional tickle? The twinge of a high note? A warm, soothing chord that washed over someone's trouble and anesthetized his or her reality? Was it a euphoric sense of being a member of a family of fans? The brief escape of identifying oneself with a charismatic personality? Or was it a real experience with God?

Whatever it was, everyone is an expert on whether or not it happened. Everybody seems to know whether the performance or message ministered to them and whether, in fact, the person doing the singing or speaking was a legitimate minister or not.

And the ministers themselves are considered a special breed. More is expected of them because they have been endowed with greater power than the average Christian. They have a higher position, a place of authority, a spiritual aura that sets them apart. It's as if some supernatural trickle-down theory is in effect and the poor, lonely guy in the fifth row has come hoping some of the blessing will manage to make its way down to him.

What's wrong with this picture?

Plenty.

First, there is no magic to ministry. No aura. No privilege. Ministry is simply *service*. Jesus Christ set the supreme example by divesting himself of all His privileges as God and humbly taking on the form of a servant. He himself declared, "For even the Son of Man did not come to be served, but to serve, and to give his life as a ransom for many" (Mark 10:45). Ministry is what you give, not what you get.

Second, there is no mystery to ministry. No intangible blessing. No spiritual goo. In fact, the Bible usually refers to ministry in very concrete terms. According to the Scriptures, it involves giving a cup of cold water, preaching the Gospel to the poor, visiting those in prison, caring for widows and orphans, and washing one another's feet. There is nothing in the Bible about singing a moving song to touch the hearts of people.

Third—and probably most important of all—there is no primacy to ministry. Nothing sets one Christian over another. There should be no sense of superiority in any ministry, because the Scriptures clearly teach that all of us are ministers. Each of us is responsible for serving according to the gifts that have been given to us. No single ministry is more important than another.

What does this understanding of "ministry" do to the Magical Ministry Tour that will roll into town next week to bless everybody? Well, it might take some of the pressure off the whole scene. It might mean that Christian ministers could be more honest, that Christian artists could present their work without having to justify it in terms of evangelism, exhortation, praise, or worship. It might mean that Christian speakers could come down off the high throne of spiritual expectations and be more human; and if more human, then more accessible to the people;

and if they are more accessible to the people, then so is the reality of knowing Christ.

After all, Christ meets each one of us right where we are, in the middle of the daily routine or the stress of indecision, in the pain of mistakes or the contentment of merely being alive, whether we're on stage or in the audience. Suddenly the Christian life could lose its mystery, become more tangible; and Christian ministry might begin to help people face life honestly rather than escape from it.

And afterward, people might even walk away more impressed with their own uniqueness and their own possibilities—their own ministry—than they were with the Magical Ministry Tour. And maybe, just maybe, they might walk away feeling bigger, not smaller.

Moses and Eleanor Rigby

*W*hat could Moses and Eleanor Rigby possibly have in common? The fictitious Ms. Rigby kept her face in a jar by the door and Moses covered his with a veil. Who knows, he might even have kept his in an urn by his bed. In public, they both wore false faces—fabricated presentations of themselves.

Every human being struggles with this problem. Have you walked into a bookstore lately and noticed all the popular books on self-awareness? Have you walked into a *Christian* bookstore lately and noticed all the popular books on self-awareness? We all try hard to present our best possible self, often at the expense of the real us.

Unfortunately, those most often in the public eye are those with the greatest propensity for wearing false faces: singers, actors, politicians, and pastors. The more promising the position, the more painstaking must be the preparation of the perfect image. Some people even go so far as to change their names.

Against this backdrop, Christians are called to maintain integrity. That's a hard thing to do, because wearing our real face in this setting would reveal the very imperfections that we cover to prove our ability. Who wants to be a human being in the company of gods? And so we wear our faces like Eleanor and cover our flaws like Moses, removing them only when we are alone and wondering who we are.

"Therefore, since we have such a hope, we are very bold. We are not like Moses, who would put a veil over his face to keep the Israelites from gazing at it while the radiance was fading away" (2 Cor. 3:12, 13). In these verses Paul reveals the reason for Moses' masquerade. He was hiding something: failure, fear, and inadequacy. We all do the same, creating a false self because we are not even sure who the true one is.

There are some people, however, who don't have this problem, and Jesus was quick to point them out for us. They are the children.

Jesus loved the little children. He told us we would have to be like children if we are to enter the kingdom of God. This analogy of the Lord's is usually taken to be an admonition toward a simple, childlike faith. But there is another aspect of children directly related to our struggle with presenting ourselves.

Little children are unconscious of self. They laugh when they're happy, cry when they hurt, and burp when they're full. My little guy has no qualms whatsoever about revealing the deepest family secrets to any listener. Isn't this what we find so appealing about children: their unconscious, unveiled innocence?

I believe it is this kind of freedom Paul is talking about when he says "we are very bold." Like a little child, Paul is not operating from a platform of self-awareness. He had found himself to be inadequate, so he quit searching there; he looked to the Lord who is adequate for all things. He realized it was not his ministry, but God's ministry in and through him. He found, just as we can, that the effectiveness of God's ministry through him continued even when he himself was failing or making mistakes.

Paul was free from self and all the accompanying masks and veils that become necessary when the self proves inadequate—and it always will. This is exactly what he meant when he said, "But whenever anyone turns to the Lord, the veil is taken away. Now the Lord is the Spirit, and where the Spirit of the Lord is, there is freedom" (2 Cor. 3:16, 17). Where is the Spirit of the

Lord? He is in us; therefore we are free!

Nothing to lose. Nothing to hide. This is the confidence that is possible in our lives when we turn from ourselves and look to the Lord. It's an open, honest, bold, frank, sometimes blunt, and almost reckless confidence. It's a *free-of-self* confidence.

"And we, who with unveiled faces all reflect the Lord's glory, are being transformed into his likeness with ever-increasing glory, which comes from the Lord, who is the Spirit" (2 Cor. 3:18, NIV). This is Paul's glorious conclusion. As we look to the Lord, He *will* be reflected out through our unveiled lives. Not only do we reflect Him today, but His reflection becomes clearer each day; more and more of Him can be seen in us as we trust Him more and more.

"Know thyself," said Socrates. Well, that's not hard. I took a good long look and found a weak, scared, inadequate, self-centered, non-caring individual. "Know thy Lord," commands Paul, in effect, "and you will begin to reflect His glorious nature through your mortal life." Even in Christ we can't fully know ourselves. We have only a small idea of what we are becoming.

Finally, notice who's in charge of the image. *He's transforming us.* He is the image-maker. It's no longer necessary to keep an extra face in a jar by the door. With the Spirit of God alive in our lives, the one we have will do just fine.

THE IMAGE

*I*t happened years ago, but I've never forgotten it. I was singing and speaking at a small midwestern college. During an informal seminar in one of the dorm lounges, a couple came in late.

I couldn't help noticing something odd about them. The girl was very attractive, close to cover-girl standards. The guy looked as if he had just walked off the set for *The Nerds*. He was short, wore thick horn-rimmed glasses and a plaid short-sleeved shirt. He was definitely a candidate for getting sand kicked in his face.

But the strangest thing of all was that these two were obviously in love. *What could she possibly see in him?* I asked myself. Suddenly I realized—she was blind.

But what did she see in him? Everything. Everything that's important about who a person is, what love is, and what a real man is. She saw everything she needed to know about him.

Blessed are the blind, for they can see people as they really are. Woe to those who can see, for they will constantly be tripped up by the *image*.

As Americans, we're obsessed with images. *Who we are* isn't

43

as important as *how we appear*. In fact, we spend so much time and effort on appearances, we lose the ability to recognize the true identity of another person, or even ourselves.

We've become more familiar with the image than we are with the real thing. How many Americans think they know football? But how many have ever been to an actual game, smelled a locker room, or even stood on the muddy sidelines surrounded by living monoliths towering over them like downtown Pittsburgh?

How many people think they know and love Robert Redford, yet they have never sat down with him and discussed his childhood? How many people think they understand Vietnam via the six o'clock news or Cambodia after seeing *The Killing Fields*? How many arrive at the Grand Canyon and are disappointed to find that it doesn't look like the pictures on the brochure? How many really know anything at all about the political candidate they voted for last November? How many news stories are actually prepackaged images created for the camera rather than spontaneous events recorded on film?

This familiarity with images spoils our relationships with real people. Instead of appreciating them for their own uniqueness, we constantly compare them to our expectations of their image.

Dating relationships are especially vulnerable to this problem. A person isn't evaluated on character or individuality, but on how close he or she measures up to the other's image of the ideal mate. Real people take second chair to the ideal; they measure up to the image or they don't.

Have you ever noticed the excitement at the beginning of a romance that later faded with growing familiarity? In the early stages of any new friendship, we're usually seeing more of the *image* than we are of the real person. We've seen enough of the surface to see similarities between the object of our affections and the ideal we seek, but not enough to show us that our ideal and the new friend are not the same person.

In essence, we're falling in love with the image, with the idea that this one person might be "it." Sooner or later the *real* person is going to start breaking through that image, and disillusionment will set in.

The success of a marriage comes not in finding the "right" person, but in the ability of both partners to adjust to the *real* person they inevitably realize they married. Some people never make this adjustment, becoming trapped in an endless search for an image that does not exist.

We'd all do well to remember the blind girl. In some ways she was handicapped. But her blindness could be a positive thing in that it forced her to encounter the unseen realities of the world around her. We are handicapped in some ways, too. Our blindness is a white blindness, a sensory overload that often shields us or distracts us from the truth.

Is it any surprise that the blind girl fell in love with the nerd? She had erased the image barrier. She saw what he was made of. Those of us with two good eyes must become more aware of how important external images have become to us and how hard we must fight to break through and get to reality.

May God grant us the same kind of sight and the same kind of blindness—that in seeing, we might truly see.

YOUNG MAN, OLD MAN, SOUP SPOON

— ACT TWO —

*T*he waitress cleared away the empty soup bowls and sloshed out two refills of coffee. "Looks like you two have been going at it again," she observed. She was accustomed to the two men at her table. They were regulars who always sat in her area because she always kept their coffee hot and never made them feel uncomfortable about staying. "What's the subject today?"

"We're still talking about sex," said the young man. He was surprised at his own abruptness. The waitress raised her eyebrows and moved on to the next table.

"No, not sex. Sexuality," corrected the old man. "The difference is the whole point of this conversation. One is what you do; the other is who you are."

"Can you clarify that?"

"Sure. Sex is something you have once in a while. Sexuality is something you have all the time—and something this generation is rapidly losing touch with."

"You've got to be kidding! My generation is obsessed with sex."

"But not with sexuality," the old man countered. "Your generation is full of sex beings but not sexual beings."

"Just what do you mean by 'sexual being'?" asked the young man. "Am I one?"

"I should hope so! Look. In the beginning God created man in His image. 'Male and female created he them.' Right?"

"Right."

"A sexual being is a man seeking to realize his maleness or a woman seeking to realize her femaleness," the old man continued. "Your generation has gotten so nervous about this that you can't even discuss it without cries of *inequality* or *sexism*. I'm not talking about roles. I'm talking about intrinsic differences, the kind you can see in the mirror."

He burned his lip on a quick sip of coffee and jerked the cup away, spilling some onto his lap. "She doesn't even give it a chance to get drinkable, does she?"

"No, not today," the young man smiled. "Not with this subject!"

"The differences in the mirror are merely the obvious ones," the old man went on, wiping off his pants with a napkin. "God didn't make man male and female just for sex. He has woven maleness and femaleness into the fiber of the universe. And He has woven maleness deep into our characters, our personalities, our emotions, just as He has woven femaleness deep into hers." The old man pointed at the waitress whisking by with a full pot of coffee. She returned the gesture with a wink.

The old man leaned into the table, and the edge of his tie slipped neatly into the coffee-filled saucer. He meant to whisper, but because his hearing was impaired it came out much too loudly for the young man's comfort. "There's a lot more to being a man than having a set of functioning privates!"

The young man smiled sheepishly at the alarmed diners in the booth next to them. "Army . . . army," he said, nodding nervously in their direction. "He's talking about privates in the army."

"Look at me." The old man leaned back but the young man was looking around the room, searching for anyone else who might have heard. "I'm old. I'm sagging everywhere. And now I see I have coffee to go with the soup on my tie. But I am no less a *man* than I was fifty years ago. For that matter, I am no less a *man* than you.

47

"Let me ask you a question," the old man continued. "After God created everything, including man as male and female, what did He say about it?"

"Uh . . . He said . . . it was good," responded the young man, his eyes still scanning.

"Well . . . is it? As a young single Christian man, is it good? Are you glad about your sexuality? Are you proud to be a man?"

When the young man didn't answer directly, his companion went on. "Let me guess; you want to say yes, but you're so frustrated about sex that you honestly can't. At this point you feel like your sexuality is more of a curse than a blessing. You're expending more energy fighting it than you are using it."

"Well . . . yes. I suppose you're right," the young man admitted. The old man had his full attention now.

"If God said it was good, then it's up to you to find out what's good about it! He's given you a wonderful gift in your sexuality. You need to take that energy and use it to serve and care for people rather than to fight it off.

"Thank God that you're a man. Begin to find out all that it means to be a man. And your relationships with women—probe them . . . pursue them. Not physically. That's too easy. But question women. Learn from them. Find out all you can about what it means to be a woman.

"Take it as a word of advice," the old man added. "I think a Christian woman would be thrilled at the prospect of getting to know a Christian man who understood his maleness. I bet most of the Christian men they associate with are either eunuchs or sex fiends acting hypocritically in light of their professed beliefs."

"You're asking me to do something that's very difficult," the young man said.

"I'm asking you to look at yourself in the mirror and not to forget what you have seen as you walk away."

"More coffee, gentlemen?" She was back again.

"No. Thanks."

"I've been thinking about the difference, and I think I have the answer," she said, resting her coffeepot on the table and adding up their bill.

"Oh, what's that?" the old man asked.

"Sexuality is the fact that I'm a woman and you are men,"

she said, leaning into the table. "Sex is what we do with it." She slapped the bill on the table and walked away.

"You know, she's not completely right," the old man said later as they were walking down the street.

"Oh, really? Sounded pretty good to me," his young friend returned.

"She gave the impression that sex was the only thing you do with your sexuality," the old man observed. "Actually, it's only one of many things. Your job is to find the others."

WHO'S O.K.?

*I*n a dressed-up culture, confidence becomes a highly valued commodity. Everything from consumer products to psychoanalysis seems designed to help build confidence and bolster ego in an "I'm O.K.; You're O.K." world.

In the midst of this justificatory jockeying for position, the Apostle Paul stuns us all with the one question we don't want to hear, for we are all afraid of where the answer might lead us: "And who is equal to such a task?" (2 Cor. 2:16). Who can really pull this off? Who is made of the stuff that can truly live up to all that we say we are and expect to be? Who can really wear the clothes well?

This is where real Christianity takes on significance. If Christians are merely selling another line of spiritual clothes to cover up human inadequacy and make us feel better about ourselves, then there is no real power in the Gospel. Anyone can go somewhere else and get a better product cover-up.

That's why Paul's question is so important; it's designed to cut through the cosmetics and show who we really are. "And who is equal to such a task?" This is what Christians need to know before dressing up for anything. It might even be why David removed his robe when he danced before the Lord.

The human tendency is to affirm our confidence, to tell God He can count on us, and like Peter, to say, "Others may fail you, Lord, but I'll never fail you." However, we all know what happened to Peter: he forsook the Lord and three times denied he ever knew Him.

The truth of the matter is we *are not* equal to the task. Those who try to be have no greater fate than Peter; the rooster crows over all our great claims of what we will do for God. Why? Because if a ministry depends on me, I will tend to present a false image of myself. If I am trying to be equal to the task, I am being dishonest about myself.

First, I force myself to avoid the whole truth about me. I mustn't tell anyone what I'm really feeling toward the brunette in the choir. I must also figure out a way to cover up the stories that are leaking out about my problems at home. I have to act like I believe God is in control of my life, when in fact I feel like it's flying apart.

Second, if I am trying to be equal to the task, I present myself as a finished product. I relegate all my problems and sins to the past, or at least they are freshly conquered. I must show myself equal to the task at all costs—even the cost of my own sincerity.

This is why Paul goes on to say, "Unlike so many, we do not peddle the word of God for profit. On the contrary, in Christ we speak before God with sincerity, like men sent from God" (2 Cor. 2:17). Real Christians are marked by sincerity—the whole truth about themselves and the whole truth about God. Real Christians stand before people the way they stand before God— transparent and vulnerable. Anything less is a dressed-up Gospel.

Insisting on the presentation of a squeaky-clean image to the world, buying into the world's system for the sake of attracting people to Christ, building spiritual empires around a charismatic personality, requiring people to fit a predetermined spiritual mold, or presenting ourselves as anything more than human beings in the process of being sanctified makes the product we peddle as illusive as worldly success. Sooner or later people will discover we are not what we claim to be. Do we peddle a glitter-

51

ing spiritual image, or do we present ourselves honestly before God and man?

Then who *is* equal to such a task? Paul doesn't fully answer that question until the next chapter, but he implies that God is more concerned with our sincerity than He is with our capability. (I have a feeling He'll take care of the second if we'll see to the first.)

Could it be that God can work through my failures? Could it be that God can receive greater glory through my confession than through my cover-up? Could it be that God's power can be perfected in my weakness? Could it be that I am not equal to this task at all, but that *He is*, if I would only release Him to work through honest confession of my inadequacy?

Could it be that I am both O.K. and not O.K. at the same time? Not O.K. in myself, but O.K. in Christ? I believe this is exactly the point the Apostle is trying to lead us to, for he answers the question by stating, "Such confidence as this is ours through Christ before God. Not that we are competent in ourselves to claim anything for ourselves, but our competence comes from God" (2 Cor. 3:4–6).

There are three important perspectives here that clearly distinguish godly confidence from false dressing up.

1. *A different audience.* "Such confidence as this is ours . . . before God." Christians stand accountable first to God. Our concern should be with what God thinks rather than what people think. The correct review of our actions is not to be found in the gossip pouring over the back fence; it is found in the Word of God and the witness of the Holy Spirit in a person's heart. Once a person has God clearly in view, the second perspective is inevitable.

2. *A different view of self.* A recent cartoon in *The New Yorker* had Christ on the cross looking down on a suited businessman and saying, "If I'm okay and you're okay, what am I doing up here?"

We aren't okay. And the one who makes God his primary audience will constantly be aware of this. There is no way you can stand before God and overlook your human inadequacies.

This is painful but liberating. People who can face and embrace their own inadequacy are the ones who are truly on the road to freedom and confidence.

"Not that we are competent in ourselves to claim anything for ourselves. . ." It first reads like an indictment but it is really a parole. We can finally face the truth about ourselves and not be afraid. We knew it all along: behind these flaky veneers of self-confidence, we are all really deathly afraid that we don't have what it takes to live.

Real Christians realize that confidence can never come from anything they are or have—talent, personality, background, opportunity—for they see themselves in the light of God. In facing themselves in that light, they are left with one glorious conclusion: they must draw from another source of power.

3. *A different source.* "But our competence comes from God." Facing our own inadequacies leads us to discover His adequacy in us. We've been looking at ourselves all along, and we finally realize we've been looking in the wrong place.

It's as if each one of us possesses a well of human resources and talents. We can operate on our own water supply for some time, but sooner or later we're going to run the pail down the shaft and hear its dead thud at the bottom of the well.

What we do at this point is the crucial issue. We can leave our empty pail at the bottom and offer people a wishing well of dressed-up illusions and facades or we can pull it up empty— willing to offer it empty at the top—but trusting that somehow He will fill it for us with His living water.

This is true godly confidence, a trust that takes us beyond ourselves, a naked confidence. It's a belief that somewhere, between the deep emptiness of our own human soul and the thirsty needs of the people waiting at the top, a strange and miraculous filling will take place. It's a confidence that operates at the risk of personal humiliation; for it believes that even if God chooses not to fill us, He has something to say through our emptiness. The only ones who ever come up full are the ones who are willing to be presented empty.

DIAMOND IN THE ROUGH

*R*eally. A King born in a stable? Who would ever look for Him there? The Creator of the universe entered human history in a dark, damp, dung-filled barn, and no one even knew, except a few who were escorted there by the hand.

We usually put nice things in nice boxes. Kings in castles. Valuables in vaults. Treasures in chests. But God put His King in a stable.

So, it isn't too surprising that He put His treasure in an equally unlikely place: "But we have this treasure in jars of clay to show that this all-surpassing power is from God and not from us" (2 Cor. 4:7).

A valuable treasure in a clay pot. At the heart of the verse is this contrast—the seeming inappropriateness of this relationship. Something so valuable in something so ordinary, right where you would least expect to find it.

In unraveling the riddle, we find the treasure is the glory of God revealed in Jesus Christ. The clay pot is the believer—you and me. The obvious incongruity of this relationship says something about us and about the power of God.

First, it tells us that human frailty is no threat to spirituality. Reconciling humanity and spirituality has long been a problem for Christians. The image of spirituality that much of Christianity has unwittingly adopted is one that requires a certain denial of our humanness. Being spiritual means being perfect, having perfect kids, having a Scripture verse for every occasion, and always rising above the situation. The truly spiritual man somehow sails through life, leaving the average person caught in the quagmire of his humanity.

But Paul gives us a different picture of ourselves. He calls us jars of clay. Now, there was nothing more common in Paul's day than jars of clay. People used them to carry water, serve food, and drink wine. Jesus once changed water into wine in jars of clay.

If Paul had wanted to imply that Christ changes our human situation, he would have put the treasure in something far more impressive—perhaps silver or gold. Today's animated preachers could then bounce on tiptoes and announce in lilting, breathy tones how God has turned us into "silver chalices" and "golden bowls."

But we're clay jars, and clay jars are fragile. Pieces of broken pottery—archeologists call them *potsherds*—are the most common find in any excavation of ancient settlements from Paul's period. The frailty of the vessel is essential to this verse. Human weakness is no threat to spirituality, but is absolutely necessary for the proper display of God's power.

"We have this treasure in jars of clay"— we have this incongruous, unlikely relationship—"to show that this all-surpassing power is from God and not from us." When people can see our human frailty and identify with it, yet still see a power in our lives, they are forced to conclude that the power is coming from somewhere beyond ourselves. The power is from God and not from us. Extraordinary power coming out of ordinary vessels directs the focus to the source of power, not the vessel.

It stands to reason that depriving people of an honest look at our humanity also deprives them of a clear look at the power of God. To display ourselves as "silver chalices" and "golden bowls" is to make God an afterthought. Others can't see past the vessel to the source of power.

It is clear, then, that God is not planning to remove us from the ordinary. He is not paving a higher plane for Christians. He plans to take us through the ordinary—and in some cases *worse* than ordinary—so that His power will shine forth in the midst of it.

Next Christmas season, as you pass by the nativity scenes displayed on front lawns and coffee tables across America, reflect not only on the King of kings being born in a stable, but reflect also on the birth of that same King in the dark, damp, dung-filled frame of your humanity, there to glisten in the hay like a diamond in the rough.

Treasures in unlikely places: a King in a stable . . . Christ in us. . . . God is master of the unexpected. He always works like this.

It is difficult to miss His presence in the midst of such a human dance. Just like the first time He came . . .

CHRIST UNDER CONTROL

*W*e've got to do something about Jesus. Tone Him down somehow. Make Him fit more into our idea of twentieth-century spirituality. Maybe it's these new translations that are causing the problem. King James's English kept Him comfortably distant, slightly removed from reality; but the new translations make Him appear so . . . well, so (cringe) . . . human.

If He was really human, then we have a big problem—then we, too, have to grapple with our humanity. Oh no, please! Anything but that! Save me. Heal me. Sign, seal and deliver me, but don't make me deal with real life. Don't tell me my everyday is a spiritual experience. Let me keep my spirituality separate from my humanity. Let me keep it in nice, neat devotional compartments so I don't have to think about how I live.

That's what is beginning to bother me about Jesus. He was so normal. Take His first miracle as a case in point. He kept a party going. He saw the wine was giving out, so He changed 180 gallons of water into wine. It almost looks like He enjoyed people having a good time. That's downright unspiritual! Christians aren't supposed to be at parties like that in the first place, much less providing the wine. I'll bet people were even dancing! This is very disturbing.

Speaking of unspiritual, He was awfully rude. Have you ever noticed how He hardly answered the question they asked? He always pricked at the harder question no one wanted to face. Why couldn't He have given the answer His listener wanted to hear just once in a while? Why couldn't He have been nice?

Especially to the Pharisees. Have you ever read what He called them to their faces? "Blind guides, blind fools, hypocrites, whitewashed tombs, snakes, a brood of vipers" (Matt. 23). That's not a very nice way to talk about people in front of their friends.

You know, it almost looks like He was purposely trying to step on people's toes. He let His disciples gather grain on the Sabbath, He touched unclean lepers, He ate dinner with tax collectors, He healed cripples on the Sabbath and then told them to carry their beds around for a while, and He was nice to prostitutes and Samaritan women.

He even expressed all kinds of ordinary, human emotions. He got frustrated with His disciples and wondered when they would ever understand. He often got tired and wanted to go away to rest. Once He slept through a terrible storm at sea because He was exhausted. He was hungry and thirsty. The moneychangers made Him so angry that He disrupted the entire temple marketplace in rage. He became lonely and depressed because no one would stay up and pray with Him in the garden. Imagine, He actually needed and longed for human companionship. And He liked kids; He put them above things that seemed more important.

He even cried. This is almost too difficult to bear. He cried at a memorial service. (Now, why did He do that? He knew He was going to raise Lazarus from the dead, that there was going to be a great victory. But He cried anyway.) Really. Christians shouldn't cry at funerals—it's evidence that they lack faith.

We really do have a problem on our hands. We can talk about what He said and about the horrible things God has delivered us from. We can praise God and talk about how Christ is coming again to take us to our eternal home, but we must downplay the way Jesus lived.

Actually, we're on the right track—satin robes, glorious

churches, impressive performances, bright spotlights, and television . . . ah yes, thank God for television. A 21-inch screen always keeps the truth out of ordinary life.

And that's really the point, isn't it? I've got to keep Christ out of ordinary life. Otherwise, I may have to face mine.

14

WHOSE SUPPER IS IT?

*I*t had all been arranged. The first ones there had found everything just as He had said, so they prepared the Passover meal, but with an undercurrent of unrest.

It was the beginning of the end. But it was not the end of the *status quo* that they feared. They had known no *status quo* for three years and had come to enjoy, instead, the freedom and security of His constant leadership.

No, they feared the return to a *status quo* existence. Uncontrollably, old questions crept back into their consciousness. Are the nets still in storage? In what condition? How will I buy the boat? What's the going price in the marketplace? Will they still be hiring tax collectors? None of the prospects were pleasing—like being sucked back into reality after an idyllic dream.

But once everybody had arrived and they were all reclining around the table, they pushed these thoughts aside, wanting most of all to remember this evening. They looked long into the faces surrounding them, their minds snapping mental pictures in the warm glow of the candlelight. They knew it would never be the same again.

It was a night for reminiscing. The first journey with Him. The first time they realized who He was. Their first time out . . . two by two.

It was a night for laughter. Well-turned phrases were turned once more. Personal idiosyncrasies were bantered about, and they each found comfort in the humor of one another's humanness. The camaraderie was strong. Three years had been a long time.

Once in a while the laughter would be uncomfortably boisterous and then, in the split-second stillness that followed, they would once again feel the foreboding undertow that pulled at their thoughts.

Suddenly, it was a night of bewilderment. "What? A betrayer on the inside? Is it I, Lord?"

"Whatever you must do, do it quickly."

Most of all, it was a night to remember—a night we're still remembering.

A cup went by . . . something about His last taste of wine until the kingdom. And then the bread. He always broke it for them, but this time He said it was His body. They winced, as He tore at it again and again, and swallowed hard as their portion went down.

Then it was deathly silent, and all eyes were on Him. He lifted the vessel and poured another cup of the deep purple liquid. Then He held it up and said, "Drink from it. All of you. This is my blood of the covenant, which is poured out for many for the forgiveness of sins."

The cup went slowly to each mouth, then passed on from hand to hand as if it were far heavier than it appeared. They would not have gone through with this had He not commanded them to do so, for they feared the taste of all that lay ahead. They wanted to stop this moment—to hold it in the cup forever. Instead, they endured slow, hesitating sips under quick glances from reddened eyes.

And then they sang a hymn and went out into the night . . .

Today in churches across America, we have somehow managed to compress this whole evening into a tiny wafer and a plastic thimble of Welch's grape juice. Instead of looking into someone's eyes, we look at stained glass or the reflection of church lights in our tiny circle of juice. The closest human contact we have in this moment is the back of someone's head.

I grew up trying to make something mystical out of this—trying to somehow find something deep and spiritually meaningful in an inch of grape juice. I see now why I found nothing: the remembrances of that first night were born amidst the warmth and intimacy of human experience, but today's Christians are barred from freely expressing their humanity.

Let's face it, humanness has gotten a bad rap from the Church for at least a few hundred years. The body is evil and full of sin, the physical world is no good, and "sex" has become a dirty word. The further we can get away from our humanity, the better off we are.

Isn't it ironic that we are trying to escape what God came to affirm? God came to be human, but we're missing our humanity by trying to be divine.

It's time to stop this silliness and run up our *I'm-a-human-being-and-I-like-it* flag. Let's allow Jesus to walk with us through all the nooks and crannies of human experience. He's very familiar with them. He's been through this before.

In fact, He likes being a human being; he thought up the idea. He created us, and then He became one of us so He could redeem us. He is still working on that very thing now, through every event in our lives—the joys and sorrows, the laughters and the tears, through the thrill of victory and the agony of defeat. He wants the words He spoke in the beginning to once again resound amid the daily reality of our lives . . . "It is good."

Is the Lord's Supper the one that's served up on a cold pew next Sunday at 11:00? What about the meal I'll have tonight with my wife and children around the table? Whose supper is that?

YOUNG MAN, OLD MAN, REVISITED

This was getting to be a habit, and a good one at that, he thought. So much of his life seemed to be spent with his peers, single people his age, all career-oriented young adults who were too old for college and too young for the married world that was waiting for them to find someone, settle down, and start living. The old man was beyond all these considerations; he had already outlived two wives and one of his own children. The young man saw him as a huge, gnarled tree, weather-beaten and left to stand among the acres of newly planted saplings who were his usual friends and associates.

"So what's the subject today?" asked the waitress. She was becoming a part of the habit too.

"Oh, I don't know," said the young man. "How about . . . uh . . . law and grace? We haven't covered that yet. That should be good for a few hours."

"Sounds boring to me," she said dryly. "I liked last week's a lot better. It had some spice! 'Law and grace' . . . sounds like a Russian novel."

"No, that's *War and Peace*," said the old man.

"All the same to me. You youngsters having the usual today?"

"The usual for me," said the old man, winking playfully.

"Me too."

"You boys don't bore each other to death, now," she said, leaving them with two fresh cups of hot coffee.

"So, what were you thinking?" asked the old man.

"Well," he said, dumping two plastic thimbles of creamer into his coffee and stirring slowly, "I've always been a pretty disciplined person and I get frustrated not being able to accomplish everything I feel I should. I know there's a balance between law and grace, but I don't seem to be able to find it very often. I mean, I'm the type of guy who will pick up other people's gum wrappers! Crazy, huh? I know about God's grace, but I'm afraid that I might take advantage of it."

The old man took a sip of coffee and maneuvered the cup on a crash course back to its saucer. "Well, first," he began, "there's nothing wrong with the Law, nothing wrong with discipline, nothing wrong with picking up gum wrappers. It all depends on where you're coming from. Some people accomplish lots of things and remain at peace inside. Others accomplish the same amount—maybe even more—but are burning up inside, constantly haunted by guilt and wondering if they're doing enough.

"It's primarily a question of identity. If your identity and worth are wrapped up in *doing*, then you will never do enough— there are a lot of gum wrappers out there—and you will be full of either pride or guilt in relationship to what you do. If your identity and worth are tied to who you are, then you have a different perspective entirely.

"For the real Christian, *being* is paramount. The issue has already been settled. Value and worth have come as free gifts from God. We cannot lift a finger to earn the most important thing. But for the legalist, *doing* is everything. He must ever try to prove that God has changed his life. One person picks up the gum wrapper out of gratitude; the other person picks it up for points."

"That makes sense," the young man interjected. "It's definitely an existential world, isn't it? 'You are what you do.' "

"Exactly," said the old man. "Ever notice how we always ask *What do you do?* when we meet strangers, never *Who are you?*"

The young man nodded approval over the brim of his cup. The old man continued. "If you're brave enough, the next time someone asks what you do, why don't you try answering, 'I live out the knowledge that God loves me and gave himself for me,' just to see what happens?"

"Now *that* would definitely stop a party!"

"Party?" The waitress appeared with two hot bowls of soup and slid them in front of the men. "I'm always up for a party. This isn't as boring as I thought." She whisked herself away, for the coffee shop was full.

The young man put a square pat of butter on top of his chowder and watched as it slowly melted away. "But what happens to the standard?"

"Nothing," replied the old man. "It remains what it has always been. Jesus came to fulfill the Law, not destroy it. In fact, it's the legalist who destroys the Law."

"Wait a minute . . . wait a minute. The legalist destroys the Law? How can that be? Law is his middle name!"

"The legalist always reduces the requirements of the Law. He has no choice but to shrink it to something that he can maintain so that when he compares himself to another, he will always win. He counts on God to grade on the curve."

The old man let that one sink in for a moment and went on, "Remember how Jesus dealt with the Pharisees? He reinterpreted the Law to them. He made it harder, putting the Law back up where it belonged. He redefined murder as hate and adultery as lust, and suddenly the old buzzards were back on the hook."

"Look out, now. Who's calling who an old buzzard?"

"Well, you're right. I wouldn't understand this so well if I hadn't been a Pharisee—an old buzzard, if you like—for a long time. The Law is supposed to condemn us. Nobody can follow it. Paul said it's the schoolmaster to lead us to Christ and I, for one, spent a good many years skipping out of that class!

"Think of it this way." And the old man started rearranging the utensils on the table. "Your soup is the City of Grace. But the only road to that city goes by my coffee here, which is the City of Condemnation—"

"Yeah, tastes like it this morning."

"—and through my soup over here, which is the City of Hu-

65

mility. The legalist is simply not willing to pass through my coffee and my soup to get to your chowder over there with the butter melting on the top—I still don't understand why you do that!"

The old man continued. "In the final analysis, there are only two types of people in the world, and believe me, they're not Christians and non-Christians. It's a different division, one that Jesus himself made. One stands on the corner in public and prays with his arms outstretched to God"—and the old man's arms went up as did his voice, much to his companion's chagrin—" 'Lord, I thank you that I am not like this man,' and points to the other who is in the alleyway, on his knees in the mud, crying, 'Lord, have mercy on me, a sinner!' That's it! Those are the two types of people. The Law has been reduced to a standard of comparison by the first man, but it has broken the back of the second. It is the one on his knees who will know the love of God."

"Does that mean you spend your whole life on your knees?"

The old man's face brightened. "Not a bad idea at all, I'd say."

"But . . . but certainly you're not saying you walk around feeling like a wretch! You just talked about a person's identity coming through God's grace."

"Yes, I did. But grace doesn't erase the Law either. You live in the tension between the two. The Law stands. You can't follow it—but you had better *try!*"

The old man stared across at the puzzled look on his young friend's face. He knew he had played his words perfectly and was ready to move in for the kill. With reminiscent flare, he removed his glasses and leaned into the table—an automatic gesture from his years of teaching that said, *If you get anything, get this!* The young man held on to the edge of the table for support.

"The Law is the schoolmaster to lead us to Christ, son, but you have to remember, CLASS IS ALWAYS IN SESSION!"

The old man pulled his soup bowl back up to his stained tie and plunged the spoon in. The young man watched him eat for a moment and then went back to his chowder, making swirls out of the melted butter. They went on to talk of other things that day, but he had already heard the most important words, and he never forgot them.

But there was another thing he never forgot about that day. As they were leaving the coffee shop, the old man had pointed to a small gum wrapper on the floor and the young man had stooped to pick it up with a big grin on his face. Looking up, he had caught a knowing glance in the old man's eyes.

It was that glance that he remembered for a long time, for it was the last time he ever saw the old man's face.

ON A DEAD RUN

*W*ith my hotel key clutched tightly in hand, I jogged through the cemetery for the second morning. Cemeteries make great early morning running: quiet, scenic, no traffic. In spite of these advantages, however, there was an eerie uneasiness that accompanied this run. I had felt it the day before as well; something to do with the respect of the dead (or lack of it), like the desecration of Indian burial grounds by the white man oblivious to spiritual sensitivities. Was it just my imagination, too many Spielberg movies, or was there something real about being in the presence of so many bones? Why did I feel like a crowd was watching me?

To compound this feeling of irreverence (a feeling I could not logically find valid), I had noticed a policeman the day before, as I exited the stone gate, who had just ticketed a commuter. He barked something unintelligible into his loudspeaker. I wasn't sure, but I thought at first that the command might have been directed at me, but I had kept on running.

So this morning, hypnotized by my rhythmic breathing and the pounding of my impious Adidas on the pavement, I lapsed into a fantasy. Recalling the previous day's encounter, I wondered what might happen if the policeman came after me today.

I imagined hearing his approach behind me on the narrow one-lane road. He followed me for a while, adding the high idle of his creeping squad car to the sense of foreboding I was already feeling from my underground audience. His tires crackled on the hot pavement. I ran on, ignoring him until he finally pulled up next to me and warned, "Jogging isn't allowed in the cemetery."

"Well . . . you can be sure . . . ," I panted, "I'm not bothering any of the residents!" (It was the kind of cockiness I have only in my fantasies.)

"Look, are you going to stop, or do I have to physically remove you?"

I pictured myself stopping, gasping for breath, then leaning my sweaty palms against the open window. "Officer . . . my best friend died last week. We used to run . . . every day . . . together. Before he died . . . he made me promise I would keep running"—and here my voice would break—"and he told me to run . . . past his grave."

Water filled the policeman's eyes. He stopped his car, got out, and started to run with me. Soon the caretaker joined us and diggers dropped their shovels and started running; then a whole funeral procession followed by a local news truck filled in the ranks.

Ah yes, so much for the Walter Mitty in me. As I left my fantasy, I found my mind turning to the subject of death. I passed two new graves strewn with hundreds of freshly cut flowers. The fragrance was deliciously sweet, but I couldn't help thinking about the awful reality that lay just beneath the surfaces of those peaceful, fragrant mounds.

We certainly do have a way of dressing up death, don't we? So much of the American way of death shields us from its horrible, but necessary reality.

It used to be that a person died at home where his friends and family had gathered around him. People saw and touched the reality. They were forced to face death: the emptiness and deterioration of a body without a soul. But in so doing, they gained a clearer picture of the material and spiritual worlds.

Today, people usually die alone in some hospital bed, and the only picture of death that friends and relatives have is a corpse fit more for a wax museum than a hole in the ground. Friends and relatives file by the body and comment, "How nice he looked, all dressed up." Nice? What could possibly be nice about a dead body?

As I rounded the far end of the cemetery, I began to wonder about the spiritual implications of this modern way of death. When the Apostle Paul talked about death to the people of his day, I'm certain they were more intimate with its physical reality than we are. When he said, "For we who are alive are always being given over to death for Jesus' sake, so that his life may be revealed in our mortal body" (2 Cor. 4:11), they must have had a painful sense of the reality of constantly facing something horrible. I think we gloss over verses like these just like our society glosses over death.

I wonder what we miss of the reality of what Christ wants to do in our lives in the process. Paul says we are constantly being delivered over to death, but who ever sees it? How many people actually get close enough to touch the lifeless death of our humanity, to experience the real life of Christ in our mortal lives? How much of what we present to people is merely a waxed corpse?

We mustn't be afraid to embrace in ourselves the loneliness, frustration, and futility of life. Even the Bible concludes that human existence is fraught with futility and emptiness, and the only reasonable thing to do is to fear God and keep His commandments (Eccles. 12:13). Certainly knowing Christ brings meaning and hope to that existence, but not at the expense of its reality.

Christ doesn't wax death over and strew its mound with freshly cut flowers. He brings life out of the midst of death like flowers up from the ground. Not the cut flowers that will whither and die in a few days, only to be replaced by repeated visits until plastic ones will do. But Christ's life grows and blooms right out of the bedrock of that which is always futile and dying in us.

If we want people to see the power of God in our lives, we will have to be willing to let them touch the frustration and death that is there as well. Otherwise we will be giving them a dressed up version of something that is actually quite grotesque.

Meanwhile, flying on a dead run, I pounded past two more fresh mounds and back through the stone gate onto the busy street to my hotel. I had to admit after all this freaky fantasy and heavy reflection, it was nice to be back on the busy, bustling boulevard.

TWO FOR A PENNY

*W*orth. What do we base it on?
Accomplishment? Applause? Prestigious recognition? Awards?
And how much effort goes into proving that we are important?
Or how much frustration is the result of wondering if anybody
noticed? Is *worth* something we have or something we achieve
by dressing up?

Christians can understand that worth is something we already have, and yet we often live as if it were something we have
yet to earn. (We have ulcers, inflated egos, and hidden insecurities to prove it.) The value of a person is not measured on an
applause meter; it is measured in the heart and mind of God.
Any believer can rest assured, for on God's scale, the needle
always reads high.

*"Are not two sparrows sold for a penny? Yet not one of them will
fall to the ground apart from the will of your Father. And even the very
hairs of your head are all numbered. So don't be afraid; you are worth
more than many sparrows"* (Matt. 10:29–31).

Three things strike me about these simple, beautiful words
of Christ. First: His will encompasses *everything* in my life. If God

wills to allow the death plunge of an innocent sparrow and can somehow incorporate that tragic event into His total plan for the world, then He certainly must be doing the same with the apparent tragedies that occur in my life. There are preachers today who present an image of God as one who stands helplessly before the unhealed, the unemployed, and the weak in faith because their lack of faith has somehow carried them away from His will. But their God is too small. Limiting God's will to what is good for me (from my finite perspective) is to rob Him of His sovereignty over all things.

Second: God is involved with us even in the most minute detail of life. The hairs of my head . . . numbered! Really! I as a musical artist am feverishly trying to get myself noticed in the world—the right picture, in the right spot, in the right magazine—so I can get myself in the right place at the right time, wondering if I should get the right manager who can do all these right things for me. But God says, "Hold still; I'm counting— 12,534 . . . 12,535. . . ." (Except that in my case, it would be— 12,534 . . . 12,533. . . !)

We are already recognized, fully known by the only Audience that matters. He knew us before the beginning of time (Rom. 8:29–30) and even prepared good works that we could walk in (Eph. 2:10). If you ever wonder whether you're getting enough publicity, just open the Bible—you'll find your picture splashed on every page.

Third: God not only knows us, but He values us highly in spite of all He knows. "You are worth more than many sparrows." My perception of this concept went through a wonderful metamorphosis as I meditated upon it. At first I wasn't very impressed. How many sparrows am I worth! Fifty? A hundred? At least a thousand, I hope! And then it hit me. Sparrows may not be very important to me, but they are very important to Him. He conceived of them in His mind and created them with great care. He fashioned them with perfect aerodynamics and set them soaring in the sky. He taught them how to gather food, to reproduce, and care for their young; and when one flies unwittingly into the invisible trap of my plate-glass window and falls lifelessly to the ground—He knows. Suddenly the worth of sparrows shot up—and so did mine, as well as the value of every person on the face of this earth.

You and I are the creatures He prizes above the rest of His creation. We are made in His image and He sacrificed His Son that each one of us might be one with Him. Sparrows are sold at two for a penny; we were bought with a much higher price.

REFLECTIONS ON AN ALIEN

I was on a plane recently when I noticed a ten-year-old boy playing with a plastic replica of some horrible creature from outer space. It had purple bat wings, long red steer horns, a pig snout, glowing red eyes, and silver crab claws for hands. Its two legs were composed of three skinless bones that joined at the ankle, forming huge eagle talons for feet.

His toy was somebody's nightmare!

It immediately started me reflecting. In a rash of fascination with science-fiction, movie producers, authors, and now even toy manufacturers have engaged their imaginations to create a wild array of alien creatures. But these other-than-human beings always seem to turn out hideous rather than beautiful.

Even E.T., whom we learned to love—at least some did—was not initially a desirable friend. I certainly wouldn't have wanted to curl up next to his crusty little body!

To what do we attribute this propensity for the macabre? If imagining something wonderful in outer space is just as easy, why don't we see more of that as well?

One possible explanation might be the innate fallenness of

man. Perhaps the effects of man's fall are far greater than we realize and our fear of the unknown brings out this subconscious malignancy.

But at the same time, perhaps we are far more *wonderful* than we realize. So wonderful that it's hard for us to come up with anything better—like dressing up a Christmas tree with tinsel, lights, and balls and then stepping back to admire it, knowing all along that it looked better growing green and tall in the forest.

Or could it be that the real reason for this tendency is that good, in fact, is not as easily accessible to man as evil? My own evaluation of art would prove this. Have you ever noticed how much easier it is to portray hate than love or bad than good, how monsters are more numerous than masterpieces, how "before" is more graphic than "after," or how sin is more alluring than conversion? Creating "downward" appears to come much more easily than creating "upwards."

In the Gospel of Mark, a man rushed up to Jesus with a question. He addressed Jesus as "good teacher," but Jesus interrupted his question by saying, "Why do you call me good? No one is good except God alone" (Mark 10:17, 18).

Herein lies our problem. When we try to portray goodness, we are venturing into a realm inhabited by God alone. We are attempting to express that which we have lost, that which is beyond our ability to create.

How then will we present beauty and goodness to the world? I believe Steven Spielberg touched upon the answer in *Close Encounters of the Third Kind*. It was one movie that presented a creature more wonderful than man. But Spielberg wisely chose not to portray the creature itself, only the wonder and awe in the eyes of its beholders; we saw not the creature, but its reflection in the faces of those who gazed upon it.

This reminds us of Paul's words in 2 Cor. 3:18: "And we, who with unveiled faces all reflect the Lord's glory, are being transformed into his likeness with ever-increasing glory, which comes from the Lord, who is the Spirit."

This is how we present God's glory to the world. We do not ape it, dramatize it, or cover it with tinsel and lights. But as we make Him the focus of our lives, we will reflect Him through what we are and what we do.

Oh, that the world might watch us watching Him and wonder at what they see!

DRESSING UP

I hate buying new clothes for myself. It always seems like there's a better way to use the time and money—like buying new clothes for my wife . . . and she agrees. But sooner or later it's inevitable. Socks wear holes and collars fray. And my wife's idea of darning socks is to throw them in the wastebasket and say, "Oh darn!" Since it happened to be my birthday, I claimed that as an excuse and had my family take me shopping.

I must confess, we didn't buy American; I purchased Taiwanese products instead. I justified it by telling myself that Americans were picking up a profit somewhere along the line. Besides, I decided, I know a lot of missionaries in Taiwan.

The first shock, which usually comes at the cash register, came earlier: I caught a glimpse of myself dressed up in the mirror. Fear of the unknown gripped my heart. *I looked good. In fact, I looked downright terrific!* I stood there torn in two, half of me wanting to enjoy it, the other half wanting to retreat to the comfort of a flannel shirt, a pair of jeans, and hiking boots.

Where does this come from—my propensity to blend into

the woodwork? My high school and college days were different. I can vaguely recall pressing my shirts in the dormitory washroom; even my blue jeans had creases then. But that had all changed in 1969 when I threw off my good-little-Christian-boy act, as best I could, in search of reality.

While angry students fought minor skirmishes with riot squads in Berkeley, I was growing my hair down to the tops of my ears and wearing my old gray-green sweater—you know, the one with the holes in the sleeves. And while my less fortunate peers were escaping the establishment's grip by blowing their minds on LSD, I had unplugged my iron and begun to wear wrinkled shirts.

There was purpose in my sloppiness. It was my own way of throwing off the demands made by my parents, church, Christian college, girlfriend . . . and even myself. It was as close as I ever came to hippiedom; hardly radical by the standards of the sixties, but it was important to me.

It even had spiritual significance. I was telling God that He had to create something in my life; I was tired of trying to do it all myself. Not realizing that this was what He had always wanted to do, I embarked on a liberating and learning experience for several years. For the next decade I wore wrinkled shirts and watched Him create.

He's done well. A lot of good things have developed on the inside—confidence, peace, hope . . . and lately even a little daring. Enough to get me into this store and put this stuff on. But was there enough to make me walk out of there wearing it?

Much of this has to do with the struggle of being a Christian artist. I've detested flashiness for a long time. I've consciously avoided anything that would draw attention to myself. I've wanted truth to shine and Christ to be seen. I had agreed with John the Baptist: "He must increase; I must decrease."

But does that really mean "He must increase; I must look sloppy"? Must I put myself down in order to raise Him up? Or in the end, am I putting Him down, too?

Maybe it's time for all that He has worked inside of me to work its way out. The wrinkled shirt may not tell the whole story. Amid the dead wood that God prunes out of a life, there is also a lot of new growth, and new growth signals its arrival with beautiful blossoms. Maybe it's finally time to present this human being as an exhibit of praise to its Creator. He is redeeming—not destroying—the value in our lives. There just could be something to celebrate here.

Well, I'm now on my third day in light-tan Italian shoes. (Maybe I should say "Italian *looking* shoes." This time I bought American.) I still give a slight shudder when I look down, but then it's followed by a growing smile—a twinge of the old fear, a rush of the new confidence.

Either I'm totally deluded or I'm actually starting to feel good about myself all the way through. I have this strange and wonderful desire to venture out of the woodwork. I don't want to blend in anymore. After all, I'm worth a whole lot to someone very important—and that's worth dressing up.

I and I—
One says to the other
No man sees my face and lives.

—Bob Dylan

PART

II

CUTTING IN

*S*o here I am. I've figured out what these clothes mean—and don't mean—and I've managed, with some difficulty, to get myself dressed and out onto the dance floor. But would you believe it, halfway into the first number some jerk cuts in on me?

Standing once again along the wall of the gymnasium, where I've stood before for different reasons, now licking the wounds of my damaged ego, I inquire as to the name of this intruder, and I find out his name is Life. They tell me he often cuts in on dancers. They also say that when he cuts in, he always cuts deep, so deep that it's almost as if you have been cut in two and one part is left staring at the other, both open and vulnerable. They say this knife can go all the way to the dividing of soul and spirit, joints and marrow, and that it can even judge the thoughts and attitudes of the heart.

CASUAL CRIMES

J boarded the plane with a Pulitzer Prize-winning book about South Africa tucked neatly in my briefcase and my purpose for going planted squarely in my heart. I was going as a prophet. I was going to direct my voice to the issue at hand: to set South Africa straight on apartheid. Those dormant protest passions from the sixties were rattling in my bones.

But self-righteous feelings such as these are always short-lived. It doesn't take long for them to crash to the floor. Mine came down—down around my ankles—before I even got on the plane. All it took was for me to see a healthy, happy, white South African couple with their two children, apparently returning to their country after a visit to the United States. I saw them as I saw myself: simply trying to survive—trying to provide a respectable life for my family and a future for my children. I realized for the first time that if the power base in their country were suddenly turned over to the blacks, they would most likely have neither.

As I watched this family in the boarding area, I thought

about the fact that much of the problem in their country has been inherited. The apartheid state was not the result of a few horrible men and women who had nothing better to do one weekend than to dream up a scheme to oppress 24 million people. It is the result of a thousand casual crimes laid one on top of another through several generations. They were "casual" because each one of these acts taken separately could probably have been rationalized as stemming from good intentions. But they were "crimes" because their effects are a totally untenable situation. Sadly, the crimes of South Africa are so deeply entangled in history that it appears impossible to unravel them.

I knew I would return from this trip a changed man, for I could already see in that nation a warning for my own life. I would return with a resolve to root out my own casual crimes before they became too deeply entrenched. It wasn't too late for me, but I didn't feel I could wait any longer.

If it's time for me, it must be time for you; for we are living in an age of dullness, an age of moral and spiritual casualness in which the distinctives of our faith have been all but swallowed up by society. We have produced an environment almost conducive to casual crimes, where it's too easy to get away with them.

But we must remember that there are consequences for all crimes, even the casual ones. This is an important part of God's order. Grace does not erase the natural repercussions of sin. When God forgives us and declares, "I will still love you," we often take it to mean "I will excuse you from the results of sin, too." But while forgiveness always restores fellowship, sin has left its wake. To make alliances with the smallest sin in our lives, to tolerate a casual crime, or to hesitate to respond to the voice of the Holy Spirit will leave a trail that we may not even see. As Paul observed, "The sins of some men are obvious, reaching the place of judgment ahead of them; the sins of others trail behind them" (1 Tim. 5:24). The trail of casual crimes follows unseen, a track that must be cut off before it begins.

Perfection is not the issue. Awareness and obedience, hearing and acting, being awake and being faithful are our concerns. A good man is not a perfect man; a good man is an honest man, faithful and unhesitatingly responsive to the voice of God in his life. The more often he responds to that voice, the easier it is to hear it the next time; the more one ignores that voice, the fainter it becomes.

There is much to do. We have our private crimes to deal with, but we also find the victims of society's crimes all around us, needing our help. It seems an endless battle from which there is no rest. False teachers will say that there is nothing more to do since Christ has already won the victory. Although that's true, although victory is sure, merely knowing that we have won this war doesn't excuse us from the battlefield. The daily battles of life must be fought until the Lord's return.

Until then, my battle is right here at 24 Green Street. It's a battle to stay awake, to avoid being drugged by my culture. It's a battle to comprehend the importance of every moment—to realize that everything matters, everything counts. It's a battle to keep remembering that I cannot dance around my responsibilities and my casual crimes without experiencing the consequences of my actions.

FEET OF GOLD

*T*he king had had a dream. "You looked, O King, and there before you stood a large statue—an enormous, dazzling statue, awesome in appearance. The head of the statue was made of pure gold, its chest and arms of silver, its belly and thighs of bronze, its legs of iron, its feet partly of iron and partly of baked clay. While you were watching, a rock was cut out, but not by human hands. It struck the statue on its feet of iron and clay and smashed them. Then the iron, the clay, the bronze, the silver and the gold were broken to pieces at the same time and became like chaff on a threshing floor in the summer. The wind swept them away without leaving a trace" (Dan. 2:31–35).

Imagine gold, silver, bronze, and iron turning to windblown chaff right before your eyes. Imagine watching and feeling the lonely desert wind eroding away the rubble from this enormous, awesome image—turning it to swirling dust.

Com´pro·mise, n. 3. The result or embodiment of concession or adjustment; hence, a thing intermediate between, or blending qualities of, two different things.—Webster's

What was it that vaporized this valuable statue? Compromise—a mixture of things that don't mix. The feet of iron and clay were the vulnerable spot of this image, causing even the strongest and most impressive of metals to disintegrate to dust.

I've been wondering lately, *How much of what is good, strong, and true do we place on feet of compromise? How much of what we are building stands on feet of iron and clay?*

That's a difficult question to answer because compromise is so hard to detect. It's slippery, illusive. It conceals itself in the highest places and wraps its evil tentacles around the bedrock of truth. It disguises itself with good intention and, when uncovered, it excuses itself repeatedly with fatalistic cries of helplessness.

Compromise is primarily a heart issue and this is what makes it so hard to discover. How do we examine the heart? Most of us are pretty much in the dark about our own heart, much less anyone else's. Paul the Apostle declared, "I care very little if I am judged by you or by any human court; indeed, I do not even judge myself" (1 Cor. 4:3). He goes on to say that he leaves the final judgment to God, the only true examiner of the heart.

Does that mean we leave compromise entirely untouched? Do we hope for the best and naively assume that everyone who calls himself a Christian acts out of deep and unquestionable integrity of heart?

I think not. Although none of us is in a place to judge the human heart, we are all in a place to call it into question—our own heart and anyone else's.

I watched a TV documentary recently on the plight of the American farmer. It was a case study of one typical farm family whose story has been repeated thousands of times across middle America.

Their situation was fairly easy to understand. Opportunists had convinced farmers to increase output for a huge international market—big profits for everyone. Farmers bought the idea, stretched themselves financially and borrowed to the hilt to prepare crops for the world. But trade embargoes and foreign policy shifts swiftly slammed the international door shut, and farmers were left with huge credit deficits and nowhere to turn. Now, despite government subsidies and farm aid, loan recalls and foreclosures are rapidly turning the farm industry into a modern dinosaur.

To make matters worse, we've discovered we can import food from other countries more cheaply than we can buy it from our own farmers. And, of course, since the profit margin is ultimately the basis for most decisions, we buy the cheaper product. But while we import food, we drive our own farmers out of business.

I watched in disbelief as the Secretary of Agriculture addressed these problems on national television. When the case of the farm family in the documentary was placed before him for comment, he first asked weakly, "Have they tried all our programs?" When the response was in the affirmative, he then came up with this classic iron-and-clay-foot response, "Well, they were just born at the wrong time." I couldn't believe I was hearing this!

What if David had said that to the fighting men of Israel whose families had been carried away by the Amalekites? "Well, sorry guys, there's nothing we can do. You were just born at the wrong time."

I would have loved to see that bureaucrat rise up at his desk, lean into the camera, and say with all the conviction he could muster, "To tell you the truth, I don't know what we're going to do, but I pledge you one thing: I'm not going to stand by and do nothing while thousands of families lose their homes and farms. I don't know what I'm going to do, but I'm willing to lose my job to do whatever I can to change this deplorable situation."

Had he done that, there would have been at least one person standing and cheering in front of his TV set.

Neil Young began his search years ago for a heart of gold. He sang:

I've been to Hollywood
I've been to Redwood
I crossed the ocean for a heart of gold
I've been in my mind, it's such a fine line
That keeps me searching for a heart of gold
And I'm getting old.*

We're all getting old, if not in years, then old in hope and longing for true-hearted people. But I'm realizing that a true

---

*Words and music by Neil Young. Copyright 1971, Silver Fiddle-ASCAP.

heart isn't even enough. It's not enough to have a heart of gold. That heart has got to stand on feet that are made of the same stuff, feet that follow that heart, that carry out its convictions. If we're going to be true, we've got to be true all the way through. A heart of gold has got to be carried along by feet of gold in order not to be blown away.

THE ELEVENTH HOUR

*I*t is the eleventh hour. My yellow pad is covered with false starts and vain ramblings—all fallen short because they lacked integrity. The problem? Right now integrity is calling me to face the ugliness and deceitfulness of my heart and I would rather write around it, not at it. Better yet, I'd like to wait until tomorrow; then perhaps these painful insights will have blown over. But I can't wait. There is no tomorrow for this; it's the eleventh hour . . . for many things.

My insurance policy is a telling example. I've committed myself to provide for and to protect my wife, but I let my life insurance policy lapse for nine months and only reinstated it at the last minute because I was about to step onto a plane headed for South Africa. If it had not been for the trip and the reality of danger, I would have let the policy go indefinitely (unknown to my wife), but I had to do something. It was the eleventh hour . . . as it is for many important things.

It is the eleventh hour for my marriage . . . I have also promised to nourish and cherish my wife, but I'm so busy with myself that I don't even notice her or her needs. When we talk, I'm the center of attention. She gladly and selflessly gives me that attention. She lavishes encouragement upon me again and again, only to watch me walk through yet another day of compromise, another day of not following through, another day of stopping short of what I really want to do and be in my life.

It is the eleventh hour for my pride . . . I don't really want to do this. No, not here. *Is this book an appropriate place to unravel my pride?* I ask. *In front of all these people?* I add. "Is there a more appropriate place somewhere else?" comes the reply. So this is the beginning of integrity. Am I to be honest only when it's pleasant? I can't wait for a less humiliating time to face this question, because there is no time to spare.

It is the eleventh hour for my Christian faith . . . A faith that has been so comfortable, so safe, yet so abstract for so long. Now when it has to mean something, will it stand the test? The largest responsibilities in my relationship with God are all His: His grace, His love, His forgiveness, His faithfulness, and His mercy—without these, it would be impossible for me to know Him. But many duties are also mine: my faithfulness, my wholehearted love, my obedience, my honesty, my confession, my repentance. No one, not even He, can do them for me. I have treaded upon His grace, used it as an excuse for laziness, and I have taken my responsibilities lightly. Expecting God to make up the difference, I have only gone halfway. I've counted on Him to bail me out—after all, someone's always done it for me before. But in spite of His great patience, even He must be growing tired.

I also realize, all too clearly, grace and mercy are for those who have tried and failed. Well, I have failed, all right, but sometimes I wonder if I've ever really tried. If I haven't tried, then I haven't earned the right to fail. Instead, I've qualified for grace with cheap failure. Never intending to do anything about my problem, I have run to grace as a disobedient son runs to his mother, to be consoled with a kind, "There, there. Everything is going to be all right."

I've also twisted my theology to incorporate my selfishness. Knowing that failure and sin lead to grace and forgiveness, I have not fought, aware that grace will be there to cover me over, I have compromised again and again. I'm hardly a Jacob. I haven't wrestled with any angels until they would bless me, and I feel my blessings are thinning out. It is the eleventh hour for my faith.

When I boarded the plane for South Africa, it was the eleventh hour for my heart. Traveling to a land that faces its own eleventh hour, I did not want to be a pawn of apartheid. I did not desire to sing nice songs about Jesus while ignoring a political system that oppresses and dehumanizes men and women who have been created in God's image. I was worried that television cameras might show me smiling with blacks while the government smiled down on the oppressed and told the world, "See. There's no problem here. Look how happy the blacks and whites are together." I would have dishonored and even degraded the Gospel by being more impressed with myself on national television than with the heart of the God who sent Christ to preach good news to the poor, proclaim freedom for the prisoners, recovery of sight to the blind, and release to the oppressed.

It's the eleventh hour and the clock is ticking. Time is never on hold. Time is almost up. It's time to act.

PILE UP

I have a terrible time bringing myself to do what I don't want to do. It shouldn't be so hard. It's a simple requirement of life—the rite of passage between childhood and adulthood—to willingly and serenely accept responsibility, no matter how difficult it may be.

I patiently walk my five-year-old through the few things that are unpleasant for him to do by telling him there will come a time when he'll have to do many such things. I always sound so grown-up when I do this. But I hear myself and wince. I fear I'm not as grown-up as I'd like to think. I still avoid too many unpleasant things in my own life.

I've been a Christian long enough to amass a string of spiritual equations that can virtually eliminate human responsibility. Lately I've been catching a glimpse of this incredible arsenal of delays, defenses, alibis, and other smoke screens I've stored up over the years to allow me to cohabit with irresponsibility. Some of them are even *spiritual*.

I've asked myself, "Human responsibility—isn't that self-effort? And isn't self-effort merely pride?" When you've got the spirit, the soul, the body, the world, the flesh, and the devil all involved, you can put a lot of responsibility on hold just by trying to figure out who's doing what!

Meanwhile, life goes on, and the things I don't want to do never go away. They pile up—one on top of the other—until they form one large, indiscriminate mound.

I think of Jesus in the Garden of Gethsemane facing something He didn't want to do. Of course, the cup of death He faced and my pile of mundane responsibilities can hardly be spoken of in the same breath, but the *principle* is the same. Somehow, He got himself to be willing to do what He didn't want to do. "Not my will, but thine be done," He prayed. Maybe I could learn something from His experience.

I certainly wouldn't learn anything from His disciples. They were asleep. They had their alibi. After trying to wake them, finding their eyes were heavy and they had nothing to say, He went back to pray. This time He said, "My Father, if this cannot pass away unless I drink it, thy will be done."

There is something very obvious here, so simple it could be missed. There was a way to make the cup of death pass away: drink it.

By drinking the cup of death, He would forever break its power. Avoiding the cup would have allowed its control over the entire human race (himself included) to continue. There was no way out but through it—and this is the important point: *through it was the way out*, the only way out. Drinking the cup of death, He conquered death and unlocked the resurrection power of God for himself and for all of us.

I'm beginning to understand that avoiding responsibilities not only allows them to continue their control over me but it compounds their power. There's no way around this pile. Oh, I can try and step around it all the time, but as it grows I have to squeeze by to get to other things. Like the disciples, I can go to sleep, but then I have to face Jesus with heavy eyes and nothing to say; and when I finally do wake up, the pile is still there waiting for me with a few more things added.

I'm tired of spiritualizing this thing. I'm tired of dragging it out. I must admit the obvious. There's only one way to get rid of this pile: pile into it.

Besides, I have a feeling there just might be some resurrection power waiting for me somewhere in there.

CLOSE SHAVE

*T*t's just an ordinary morning in the bathroom . . . but this morning I find myself reflecting on my crumpled, almost spent, Gillette brushless shaving-cream tube.

As I study this twisted mass of metal, hardly recognizable anymore as a useful toiletry, I'm impressed with a simple observation: *This is not my doing. I don't treat tubes like this—any tube.* I push the contents up from the bottom, even roll up the empty part, to keep a nice, neat mass of shaving cream readily available near the top where it belongs.

It's obvious that this poor tube has been indiscriminately grasped in someone's hand and crushed beyond reason. What's more, a significant amount of its contents has been expelled, certainly far more than the sparing amount I usually extrude to shave with every day.

I have reason to suspect my wife.

I look in the bathtub and my suspicions are confirmed. Large lumps of waterlogged shaving cream clog the drain like cottage cheese in a kitchen sink. It looks like three, maybe four of my shaves have been luxuriated on her legs. Ten years of continuous lectures on the use and abuse of shaving cream have obviously fallen on deaf ears.

Appraising the aftermath of this indulgence, I find myself unable to ward off a number of disquieting thoughts. *Maybe I should hide the tube, hoard my own little stash of personal items. I don't have to put up with this.*

But then, I remember when I was single. *Ah, yes! Everything just as I wanted it, where I wanted it. No wife smearing shaving cream all over her legs. No little children finger painting it on the shower walls.*

And finally, *What would it be like to be married to someone who treats a tube with the same respect I do?*

This last thought shocks me back to reality. I can't believe I'm thinking these things! I'm allowing myself private thoughts of disentanglement because of a beat-up shaving cream tube. As I squeeze, roll, and pound the stiff metal, trying to free the last few globs for my rapidly drying beard, I realize this little tube has revealed a desire on my part to not completely "own" being married.

My reflections turn to thoughts of ownership. If I don't completely own being married, then I don't have to own the problems associated with it. They're not mine, just like this tube is no longer mine. Financial problems, for instance, are the results of taking on the responsibility for a wife and kids. I had always kept my books in order before they came along.

I pursue the idea, squeezing out the painful ramifications. *How deep does this go? I'm not sure I want to know. How many of my problems have I refused to own, finding it much easier to place the responsibility on someone else?*

And what of sin? I wonder how much of sin's work I've overlooked in my life because I've refused to call it my own.

I stare into the bathroom mirror, the last of the shaving cream beginning to rapidly crust on my face, and the revelation flows like water from a faucet. *If I haven't owned my sin, then the forgiveness isn't mine either. If I haven't owned the pain in life, then I probably know little of true joy. If I haven't owned this marriage—the problems, the finances, the disagreements, the wasted shaving cream in the drain—then I'm not fully experiencing what it means to be one with my wife.*

I stare at the man in the mirror. I've looked at him so many times before; but this time I look deeper into his humanity and find him becoming uncomfortable, on the brink of turning away. He's fighting within himself—sure of what he must do but not sure he can do it.

Suddenly, he looks me square in the face and speaks. "Hi. I'm John and I'm a sinner. And if it wasn't for the grace of God, I wouldn't be standing before you this morning."

That confession is greeted with a sudden burst of applause in the room. New confidence floods him as he grabs a wrinkled-up red-and-white tube from the sink. He steps up onto the children's potty chair and clutches the tube tightly to his chest as if receiving an Olympic medal. Then he holds it up in front of himself reverently and speaks again. "And this . . . this beautiful mess of metal . . . this is *my* tube!"

There's more applause; and it seems it will never cease—because, after all, it's just the water running in the bathroom sink.

SOUL TALK

Praise the Lord, O my soul.
O Lord my God, you are very great.
(Ps. 104:35)

What is this greatness that outshines all of my earthly existence? Someone out there is much greater than I. How can I begin to understand this? All I know is what I see, feel, touch. I am the center of this discovery; it works out from me and I try to see it from here, but can I?

My life centers on the tangible; I am survival-oriented, self-revolving. How can I see beyond me? So often it seems my graspings for this great One fall short of my own fingertips. Don't I need to go beyond myself? Don't I need to take some mystical journey on the chords of a pipe organ or the vibrato of some holy voice, or be carried into spiritual realms by the ecstatic utterances of men and angels, or take some pilgrimage to a mountain retreat to encounter God's greatness in the solitude and grandeur of His creation?

Is it that unattainable, or is it possible I could find God's

98

greatness right here? Can I find it in the last, cold swallow from my coffee cup? Or on the messy desk, full of my daily ramblings—attempts at organization fallen short in the junkyard of good intentions? Can I find this greatness as I rush downstairs to the noise of the garbage truck at the neighbor's house, knowing I have just enough time to get my cans out, the ones I forgot the night before? Can I find it here in the Bible lying open on top of my unfiled folders, in Psalm 104, an ancient manuscript of a man—like me—trying to understand the greatness much greater than he? But no, not just understand it, to touch it, to know it, to have that greatness become a part of him, a part of his deepest part: a part of his soul?

"Praise the Lord, O my soul."

Who is he addressing here, anyway? I've heard he was a shepherd. Was he talking to the sheep—his captive audience on a clear Palestinian night? Was it the great assembly of the nation of Israel after he became king? Was he thinking of all the people who would read this when he said, "Praise the Lord, O my soul"? The pastor brushing up on a sermon late Saturday night, the clinical worker on a coffee break, the seminary student picking it apart in the Hebrew lexicon, the missionary translating it into Swahili, the nun in the convent, the senior citizen on the park bench in the midday sun, or the choirs in a thousand choir lofts of a thousand churches in front of a thousand pieces of stained glass? Was he thinking of the Praise the Lord Club when he said, "Praise the Lord, O my soul"? Was he thinking of me?

O my soul—he was talking to himself! I'm privy to a man's inner conversations here. This is the kind of thing people can be sent away for! This man is carrying on a dialogue with himself: "And so I say to my soul, 'Soul, you praise the Lord.' "

Well, this may be a bit crazy but it is cause for encouragement, for apparently David had the same difficulties I have trying to touch the greatness of God in the middle of daily existence. He found he needed periodic discussions with himself—to issue directives to his soul.

What kind of soul is this? If it's a spiritual soul, he could put it on automatic pilot. If it's an ordinary human soul, he's going to have to whip it into shape. Would his soul praise the Lord if he didn't tell it to? No—nor would mine. I think I like this man. This isn't someone chiseling on the rock of ages for generations to come, nor is it the greatest hymnwriter of all time knocking out one more tune for the Jerusalem Choral Society; this is someone like you or me simply getting through another day. This is David trying to awaken his soul to the greatness that lies in the cold coffee, the cluttered desk, and the clanging garbage truck of his day.

This tells me that praise is not so much a "getting out of" as it is a "getting into" life. If God sent His Son into the world, then God's greatness is at hand. The kingdom of God is here somewhere on my desk and in the daily ramblings of my life. I don't have to go anywhere to get it. I only have to wake up my soul to see it.

There's nothing mysterious about all this, no magical key that unlocks the floodgates of praise. Nor is there anything automatic—some kind of spiritual wind-up soul that runs for a few days after being wound tightly by a praise service.

No, what we have here is an ordinary soul that needs a good talking to from time to time. Something like:

"Soul, praise the Lord. There is comfort in the coffee, destiny on the desk, goodness in the garbage. Wake up, O my soul! Listen to me, I'm talking to you. Stop trying to change the subject. You what? You already know this? Well then, how come you're not doing it? Look, soul, are you in this thing or not? This is not a nice to-do. This is life! Praise the Lord, O my soul!"

ONE DRINK AWAY

*M*y pastor is an alcoholic. I say "is" because an alcoholic never ceases to be one. Alcoholics are never "cured"; they simply decide to stop drinking . . . and it's a daily decision. An alcoholic who has stopped drinking is always—at any time—one drink away from going out of control.

For these people there is no such thing as drinking in moderation, nor is there a sense of being beyond danger. My pastor has not overcome some huge personal adversity from which he can rise up, dust himself off, and get on with life as if the problem were over. He must acknowledge that his battle begins afresh every day.

There is something terribly right about this—not about being an alcoholic—but about acknowledging our inadequacy and realizing that our struggle with sin is very similar to an alcoholic's struggle with drinking. It's never over.

I often find myself talking about sin in the past tense as if sin is something beyond my present experience, a page I've already turned in the book of my life. But sin is like alcoholism.

Sinners are never fully cured; they simply decide to stop sinning . . . and it's a daily decision.

In Galatians, Paul warns, "Brothers, if someone is caught in a sin, you who are spiritual should restore him gently. But watch yourself, or you also may be tempted" (Gal. 6:1). Notice that the one who is "spiritual" is not exempt from a fall, but is susceptible to the same temptation from which the other is being restored. We cannot rest on our spiritual laurels. We are all one drink away from being out of control. Therefore, "Watch yourself."

"But being an alcoholic is so much worse . . . ," I tell myself. "So much stigma attached to it . . . so many lives and families ruined. I get off easy, don't I? I'm no alcoholic."

Or am I?

Do I have any less of a problem than the alcoholic just because no one's organized a Lustful Thoughts Anonymous. Is being mastered by selfishness a lesser evil than being mastered by drink? Actually, the only difference between my pastor and me is that I can hide my propensity for drunkenness; and for that reason, mine is even more dangerous.

He can't go back to drinking without revealing it in his face, his mannerisms, his lifestyle, and his absence at AA meetings. I, on the other hand, can be drunk with hidden sin and no one will know for a long time. They won't even miss me at church because, unlike AA meetings, I can get away with deception at church. I don't have to worry about being found out at church because no one else wants to be found out either. We're easy on each other; we all put our best foot forward and we're all hiding—from the pastor on down.

That's what I like about AA meetings. The word is out. Everyone knows it. They all have been deceiving themselves and everyone else, but now they can't get away with it anymore. Everybody is there because they're alcoholics who want to do something about it. They have to get help because it's too big to handle by themselves.

Sound anything like what Christian fellowship ought to be? "If we claim to be without sin, we deceive ourselves and the truth is not in us" (1 John 1:8). "Therefore confess your sins to each other and pray for each other so that you may be healed" (James 5:16).

My pastor knows this reality. For every time he steps in front of his congregation and opens his Bible to speak to them from God, there was another time earlier in the week when he mounted a lowlier platform in front of another congregation and proclaimed, "Hi, I'm Frank, and I'm an alcoholic." To which a chorus of gruff blue- and white-collar voices replied in earthy unison, "Hi, Frank," as if to say, "You're one of us. We understand. We need each other."

People at the local AA meeting know what it's like to be at the bottom; they know what they have to do to stay above it, and they know how much they depend on each other to help them. When you compare the gut-level group dynamics of an AA meeting to a punch-and-cookies get-together in the fellowship hall after church. . . . (Need I say more?)

Yet this same identification is the essence of real fellowship— knowing what it's like to be a sinner, knowing the grace and forgiveness that meet us there, and knowing how much we need each other's encouragement and accountability. It's impossible to have real fellowship without sharing the common bond of our sin as well as our forgiveness.

Yes, there is a bond in sin that strips away pride, rank, social status, and religion, leaving us all in touch with a common need for our Savior—a sort of Sinners Anonymous, if you will.

Fellowship begins to make sense only in this context. Fellowship means something to saved sinners; it doesn't mean a whole lot to sanctimonious saints. Saved sinners know that a constant struggle with sin continues even after their salvation. But there is real life in this tension: grace, humility, friendship, pain, forgiveness, sorrow, and laughter.

Next time you go to church (or if you're a Christian leader, the next time you get up to minister), go with the attitude that the word is out. Everyone knows it. You've been deceiving yourself and everyone else, but now you can't get away with it any longer. You're there because you're a sinner and you want to do something about it—and you've got to have help because it's too big to handle by yourself.

My pastor is always one drink away from being out of control . . . and so am I.

And so are you.

"Let him who stands take heed lest he fall."

WE ALL FALL DOWN

I recently learned that a man whom I know and respect, a long-standing elder of a strong church, a gentle and kind man, a seeming bulwark of spiritual maturity, has been secretly living in adultery for ten years and embezzling money from friends and associates. Now I'm sure everyone has heard of this kind of thing happening, but when it happens to someone you know well, the emotional and spiritual impact can hit you like an earthquake.

The emotional and spiritual impact of this scandal can be earthshaking. The ground of your own stability rocks and you suddenly feel sick to your stomach. Questioning your ability to spot authenticity, you wonder if anyone else was deceiving you.

After shaking your head for a few days, you begin to detect a twinge of *self-righteousness* in your shock and disbelief. Your head shakes slower and the this-kind-of-thing-could-never-happen-to-me thoughts reveal the thin ice upon which your friend has stood. But slowly you become aware of your many little compromises with sin and the careful rationalizations you had made to smother the Spirit's conviction in your own life.

This man's fall was not the result of one wrong move. It was the result of thousands of bad choices, each one placed on top of the last until the voice of the Spirit had become muffled. And suddenly, the unthinkable became reality. He wasn't an evil man, only an ordinary man whose conscience had been deafened by his compromises. And what happened to him isn't so far away from any one of us.

In thinking about him, I've been led to 2 Peter, chapter 2. Peter tells us that God rescued Abraham's nephew Lot and called him a "righteous man" (2:7–8). Lot . . . a righteous man? Who are we talking about here? The same Lot who was prepared to sacrifice his daughters to the sexual whims of Sodom? The same Lot who chose the best land rather than leave it for his Uncle Abraham; whose disobedient wife was turned into a pillar of salt, and who drank himself into a stupor when his daughters wanted to have sex with him to insure descendants for the family name?

Righteous Lot? I always thought Lot was a *bona-fide* jerk! Were it not for Peter's comments in this passage, I'd have had Lot burning away in hell a long time ago. Apparently God knew something about Lot's heart that I don't see in the Old Testament account. Actions don't always tell the *whole* story.

Nevertheless, we're very quick to judge a person by externals. If someone is caught in a sexual sin or gets a divorce, we cross them out of our address book. But fortunately for Lot, I'm not his judge; and fortunately for me, you aren't mine.

We can't see deep enough into a person, not beyond the level of action. Only God can judge perfectly, seeing the hidden motives of the heart. If we could see cut-away views of the heart, I can imagine a person caught in sin revealing a righteous heart but weakness of the flesh. At the same time, I can imagine a person with an impeccable exterior shell whose heart would reveal filthiness and greed.

Whether my friend is a snared believer or an evil imposter isn't for me to decide. The bottom line here is to allow God to be the judge. Only then can I be freely compassionate, forgiving, understanding, and helpful. Only then will I truly honor Paul's instruction: "Brothers, if someone is caught in a sin, you who are spiritual should restore him gently. But watch yourself, or you also may be tempted" (Gal. 6:1).

COMING LOOSE

*J*ust inside my back door is a two-by-three-foot section of the kitchen floor where the tiles have come off. These tiles are the old-fashioned brick variety: flat red, charming, and very fragile. Some of the tiles in the center of the floor are cracked, but they are locked tightly into the symmetry of neighboring tiles and refuse to come out. Only the ones by the back door, on the edge of the flooring, are susceptible to breaking away. They have one edge exposed, very vulnerable to a variety of everyday kitchen and back-door hazards, from high heels to rolling appliances.

We have lived in this house for three years, and during this time the section of red-brick fatalities has widened by three rows. I say "rows" because that is the way it happens . . . one tile in the middle of an exposed row breaks loose and leaves its neighbors with two sides open to attack. Each subsequent casualty leaves its neighbors thus exposed until the whole row is gone. It's a domino theory: once the row starts to go, it's only a few days before all the tiles have fallen out of rank.

So far we're five rows down and holding.

I had a dream last night. Over half the floor was gone. I think this would qualify for an adult nightmare—the eroding away of something I thought was permanent. My childhood version of this same dream was to lose my teeth—the permanent ones. I rushed downstairs in the pre-dawn darkness to find my kitchen floor unchanged: five rows down and still holding.

But the dream is much closer to reality than I would like to admit. I feel that much of my life is coming loose.

Take, for instance, the idea that God is on my side, that He isn't going to let any harm touch me, that He, in fact, is my protector and rescuer from all things. If I blow it, He will always cover me. More often than not, this translates into God pulling me out of a jam. If I still think that's true, I'd better wake up to reality because *that* row came loose some time ago.

How about the idea that I'm special? God has bestowed on me exceptional gifts and talents for which He has big plans. Therefore I get special treatment and extra protection; I'm shielded from the ordinary burdens of life that everyone else has to deal with. Like a quarterback with weak knees, I get a strong front line. I am excused from having to be a well-rounded athlete as long as I can still throw the ball. (Oh great! Just what the world needs. A spiritual Joe Namath—with the appropriate arrogance to go with it!)

I am special; God has given me unique gifts and talents. But none of these things are exclusive. When God handed out gifts and worth, He distributed them to everybody. No gift comes with any privileges and each of them comes with the responsibility to use it wisely.

So much for those rows of tiles . . .

There's also the assumption that a Christian with my history and pedigree will certainly never face such personal catastrophes as divorce, despair, isolation, abdication, or suicide. These thoughts will never even enter the mind of a noted Christian like me.

Well, look into the mirror, Fischer, and welcome yourself to the human race. Stick a pin in your finger—is this anything like a nail in the hand?—and what color do you bleed? Look out at the rest of the bleeding world, at the bleeding Savior.

Do you think He ever felt like this? Can you assume you never have to know the despair of being human?

Say goodbye to another row . . .

There's even Adam's curse: "Cursed is the ground because of you; through painful toil, you will eat of it all the days of your life. . . . By the sweat of your brow you will eat your food" (Gen. 3:17, 19). Well, that doesn't apply to me. That's part of the *old* covenant. The new covenant has redeemed all that—and it's been redeemed without me ever being a part of it. It's been freely placed into my hands and I don't have to earn it in any way.

Wait! What's that? Redemption from the curse happens only by accepting my responsibility to work out my salvation? That work, that pain and toil, can actually be a sacred privilege? You mean it's my responsibility to redeem all of my human activities by entering into them with the power and purpose of Christ in me? Is that what this is all about? Building my house on a rock?

Is this His voice I hear? I'm not sure because it's been so long since I've heard Him this clearly. Shhh! It *is* His voice! Listen. He's speaking again. (Pause) I thought that was what you said, Lord. (Sigh.)

I suppose you want to know what He said. It was just a simple message. He said, "Fix the floor."

Like most of my writings, I read this one to my wife when I completed it. She was overjoyed. The kitchen floor was finally going to be fixed! But when nothing had been done by the end of the next day, she questioned me. "Why haven't you done anything about the floor yet? I figured that if God had spoken, there would be some immediate action."

"Well," I explained, "He didn't mean to actually fix the floor. I mean, there are a dozen more important things I need to get to first. The floor was just a symbol."

"Oh really?" she said in a sarcastic tone. "You mean you only write articles about these great revelations? In the meantime, who's going to fix the floor?"

Well, I'm proud to say, the floor is finally fixed. I'd like to say it was easy and fun, but it wasn't. The adhesive securing the tiles seemed to take an eternity to set and the grout smeared; but then again, overcoming bad habits, perpetual denials, and comfortable excuses is never easy. Sometimes following the Lord is a lot like fixing the floor.

FLIGHT 50

*E*very time I fly across the country, especially east to west, I can't help but think that people used to make this trip in wagon trains. Imagine the hardships they faced—the months of travel in this untamed land with its steep mountains, snowy passes, drought-stricken plains, snakes, wild animals, sun, rain, mud, rivers. Consider the Indian attacks, the primitive medical supplies, and the disaster of broken wagons or wounded horses. And the guy behind me in 30G is complaining about the person in 29G whose hat is blocking his view of the in-flight movie!

I try to remember these things when I am tempted to complain about such imaginary hardships as sitting in the middle seat of a DC-10 with two sleeping bodies between me and the freedom of the aisles on either side. I try to remember those real hardships when I can use my passenger light while the cabin is darkened for the mid-morning transcontinental movie.

I have to admire the woman in the window seat across the aisle. She's the only one refusing to close the curtain on her window despite repeated requests by flight attendants to do so.

Hazy light from the lonely oval streams in on her row of airline seats and slightly diffuses the color tones on the movie screen. I'd like to believe that she does this to maintain some contact with reality outside this screaming silver bullet.

Ground. Although at 37,000 feet it resembles something from Rand McNally rather than the creation of God, that ground is the sole indication that we are moving at a high altitude and a very high rate of speed.

I like this woman. If I had a window seat, I'd keep the curtain up, too. Something in me wants to go over there and applaud.

Maybe it's because this airplane scene somehow represents my life. That woman and I with her seem to be fighting for one small window of hazy reality in the middle of an airborne Hollywood fantasy. The darkened plane, the filtered air, and the darting, flashing celluloid all pull me into someone else's story, someone else's reality.

Somewhere below me is the truth. Somewhere down there I can walk and smell the pungent sage as it is crushed under my boots. Somewhere down there I can taste the dirt and feel the wind on my face. Somewhere down there I can feel the sun dry my lips.

"I am the way, the truth and the life," Jesus said. "But what is truth?" Pilate asked, and Jesus gave no reply. So I'll ask you. What *is* truth? Does it crack your lips? Does it catch in your throat and make you cough? Does it stick to the soles of your shoes? Does it put you in front of life's Pilates without an answer because the answer is so obvious—yet so hard to explain—that you choose to let the silence speak?

Or have you, like most of the people on Flight 50, pulled down the window curtain and let someone else create your reality? And have you done this simply because a flight attendant told you to? Oh, there's truth here, but it's someone else's truth first—if it ever is ours—and it's as far above the ground as I am right now.

I was on the ground once. I traveled this great country in a sports car with a backpack strapped to the trunk. I took back roads in Georgia and talked to old men at country stores. I drove by belching factories in Detroit and camped under the stars in the pine forests of Tennessee. I hiked the craggy mountains of southern Texas and slept on a cliff over the Rio Grande while a full moon rose on my left and a full sun went down on my right. And the dry wind chapped my lips.

But now my lips are smooth. The air is controlled in this plane just as the experiences are. Compromise has been laid upon compromise until my last touch with my heart is this one small window—a porthole of truth—and the defiant woman who guards it.

Cheer the woman. Stand in front of the screen. Open the curtains. Scream. Do something to wake up before we all fall asleep watching the movie on Flight 50.

LITE CHRISTIANITY

*T*hirty percent less trials. Forty percent less affliction. Fifty percent less confusion. Seventy percent less pain. For those who prefer a Christianity that's less filling than the regular commitment, we recommend . . . *Lite Christianity*. It's everything you've always wanted from God . . . and less."

For many people today, popular Christianity must sound something like this. And why not? We have light beer, light yogurt, light wine, and even light rock. It was only a matter of time before the Christian experience would be watered down and offered in a more culturally palatable form as well.

It's no wonder that we seldom hear verses like these: "We are hard pressed on every side, but not crushed; perplexed, but not in despair; persecuted, but not abandoned; struck down, but not destroyed. We always carry around in our body the death of Jesus, so that the life of Jesus may also be revealed in our body" (2 Cor. 4:8–10).

This isn't light at all. This is full strength life thrown at the believer with full force. Conflict, pain, and struggle form an

113

integral part of the Christian experience—not just for some, but all. The Apostle Paul here explains that the life of Christ is constantly being displayed amid the dying experiences of our mortal lives. He even restates this principle in the next verse—in case we missed it the first time. "For we who are alive are always being given over to death for Jesus' sake, so that his life may be revealed in our mortal body" (v. 11). Notice the word "always." These struggles are a normal part of the believer's daily life.

Four areas of struggle are mentioned in this passage. Believers can expect them all.

1. *Pressure.* We all feel this. It may be financial, emotional, vocational, or the pressure of responsibility in a relationship. For me it's life in general. I grew up as part of the Woodstock generation—a generation that was going to avoid the painful entanglements of the establishment. Now as a husband, father, homeowner, and taxpayer, I frequently find myself jumping into bed, grabbing my wife desperately, and crying out: "Does anybody out there really know what they're doing?"

2. *Perplexities.* There are so many things we don't understand. Someone loses a job. A close friend loses the faith. We're uncertain about an important decision. These are the ordinary perplexities of life, times when we find ourselves caught between answers, times when we put on a coat, walk out into the night, stare up into the heavens, and cry, "Why?"

3. *Persecutions.* No, the guns aren't at our heads (at least not yet), but the believer will know persecution. The price is paid in subtle ways, by social ostracism or discrimination at work. For some it may mean losing a job or a better position because of a stand against unethical practices. Students may be harassed by an unbelieving teacher because of their faith. My wife was recently ridiculed for her friendliness—a God-given quality that she is free to express, but an attribute held in suspicion by a defensive world not free to receive or understand it.

4. *Calamities.* These are the real back-breakers: serious illness, death in the family, divorce, or mental breakdown. Sometimes the calamity means falling into a sin we never could have imagined ourselves committing. These are the times when God does His deepest dredging, bringing us to a place of utter helplessness. In these times, God performs open heart surgery, cutting out pride and independence.

For each of these struggles there comes a corresponding expression of the life of Christ to preserve us, showing Him to be as real as the pain. He says we will not be crushed in the pressure. We *will* feel the pressure on every side, but we will not cave in under it, because His life sustains us.

We will be perplexed and confused at times, but we will never be utterly without hope. The question we throw out into the night will be answered. "You do not understand, but I do. I am in control. Trust Me."

We will face persecution, but He will never leave us alone. Though rejected by man, we are never abandoned by God. We will always know His eternal presence in our lives; and when we are struck down, we will not be destroyed. "Down, but not out." Finally, even in death itself, there is ultimate victory. Through Christ we are indestructible.

Lite Christianity? Far from it.

If you want a less filling yogurt, fine. Go for the light stuff. But if you buy "Lite Christianity," you're going to get just that— a much less filling experience.

CUTTING IN

*T*here is . . . a time to be silent, and a time to speak" (Eccles. 3:1, 7). This is a time to be silent.

Oh, there are so many things to say. I know them well. "God knows what He's doing and He's in control." "The baby aborted itself because it wasn't healthy in the first place." "Maybe your wife's too old to have children. It's risky after 35, you know." "The pain will make you a deeper person . . . draw you closer to the Lord and to each other."

Reasons. We always have to have reasons. They may even be true, but like the words of Job's friends, they never reach far enough to touch the pain.

It's not easy giving birth to death. I just watched a surgical Hoover evacuate the remains of our fetal hope into a plastic bag while a nurse hid the scarlet evidence and joked to cover the tension. But nothing covered my wife's humiliation.

This is a time to be silent. Why is it that we always have to have something to say? Sometimes we need someone to sit next to us and stare at the ground or kick at the darkness.

"[There is] a time to weep and a time to laugh" (Eccles. 3:4).

Jesus wept. He wept over the death of a friend and over the loss felt by the survivors. There are as many reasons for this as there are New Testament commentaries, but it's really not that difficult. Jesus wept because it was a time to weep.

If there are times to weep, I must be missing a lot of them because I've had only a few in my lifetime. I envy my children for this. Their tears flow so freely and laughter is always so close behind.

The psalmist says that God collects all our tears in a bottle (Ps. 56:8). My bottle must not be very full. But it's not because I haven't had anything to cry about; I think it's because I don't let life touch me. The tears are there, collected in a guarded reservoir somewhere behind my eyes, but gradual spillways keep the floodwaters under control.

This was a time to weep.

"[There is] a time to mourn and a time to dance" (Eccles. 3:4).

Mourning is different than weeping. It's coupled with dancing, which gives it a sense of celebration—a celebration of sadness. Weeping is sudden response, mourning is planned; weeping is spontaneous, mourning is scheduled.

Old Testament prophets tore their clothes and covered themselves with ashes to mourn the sins of the people and beseech the mercy of God. During Jesus' time, mourning the death of a loved one lasted seven days. Professional mourners were even hired to inspire grief.

These practices may not be transferable to our Western culture, but there's something we can learn from the intent. Mourning is meant to let grief run its course, give it some visible expression, and celebrate sadness. But we're so quick to resume the clatter of daily life that we never let our hearts know what really happened.

There's something else important about mourning. It's not an unending action. This is true for all three of these responses; life isn't all silence, weeping, or mourning any more than it's all talk, laughter, and dance. Each feeling gives the other a context, room to breathe, a reason to be.

There's a time to get up, wash our faces, put on fresh clothes, and join in the dance. But could it be that without really mourning, we may never hear the music of the dance?

117

*The words of the prophets are written on
subway walls
And tenement halls . . .*

—Simon and Garfunkel

PART

TURNING OUT

*W*ell, here I am. I'm out on the floor again and I can hear the music starting up. Great! I think I'm finally ready to dance. But wait a minute . . . this isn't a floor; it's asphalt! Good grief, we're out on the street!

Oh no, I don't think I signed up for this. I thought this was going to be a nice, controlled Christian dance in the church gymnasium—you know, a lot of nice Christian folks from similar backgrounds finally getting to do what we couldn't do when we were younger. We were going to have a nice clean time dancing to Christian music—no sexual dancing, of course—just something like sanctified aerobics.

This isn't fair! Somebody turned my nice, safe party out into the streets. Who are these people, anyway? I feel so strange here. The music's loud, the costumes are bizarre. I can't tell if these people are laughing or crying. Should I be around them? . . . What if I get some incurable disease?

This isn't safe; this definitely is not safe. I thought this was going to be an entirely different dance.

WHERE'S THE GRAFFITI?

I heard about a secular artist who played at a Christian college once. After he had left, someone discovered that he had scrawled "Where's the graffiti?" on the clean white wall of the backstage bathroom.

It was a poignant question. Are the walls around us really that clean? Wouldn't it be just like a prophet to mess them up like this?

The prophets of the Old Testament seemed to have this irritating quality about them: they scribbled on everybody's walls. I'm sure Ezekiel's quaint little street theater, with his shorn hair arranged in piles while he removed some of his clothes and cooked over cow dung, was a shocking bit of graffiti on the immaculate walls of social and religious propriety. The Holy Spirit himself ruined Belshazzar's feast by writing on the wall a message of doom with an invisible hand. John the Baptist carried on the tradition by living like a madman in the desert and casting a verbal ax at the foot of the sacred trees of the Pharisees. Jesus, in His first speech in the Nazareth synagogue, so infuriated people that they drove Him out of town and would have thrown

Him off a cliff if He hadn't slipped away. Something He said must have disturbed them!

The most disturbing thing about all that we say to each other in the Christian world today is that no one is disturbing anyone. There's no graffiti on the pure white walls of our Christianity. There are a few disturbing voices, but they are not necessarily the right kind of disruption. There will always be self-righteous preachers railing us and demanding that we scrub our walls even whiter. We've gotten used to the din of their voices and the resulting emotional swell of guilt that drives for relief once again upon the gentle shore of grace.

But by and large, we busy ourselves making each other feel good. We're rich, we're full, and we're saved while two-thirds of the world is poor, hungry, and hell-bound. I often look at the neat, clean walls that surround our protected world and wonder, "Where's the graffiti?"

Some might contend that the recent downfall of a major teleevangelist could be considered writing on the wall for modern Christendom, but I don't think that will prove to be the case. This does not qualify as real graffiti because there has been no real confession, just admission of a *faux pax*, a major slip-up, but something that can be put behind us. We allow events like this one to quickly wash away from our attention because we do not want to face the graffiti on the walls of the offenders; but neither do we want to face our own. Thus the modern Christian world continues its road to success, influence, fun, and profit.

But where's the graffiti? Where's the human side of our spiritual message? Where's the reality? Is the pain and hunger of the world really touching us? Do we force ourselves to see? or does being a Christian mean I don't have to encounter this anymore?

I'm afraid we have led ourselves to believe just that, for we are continually whitewashing the writing on the walls of our environment. But living in a whitewashed world is not what Jesus intended for us. In the garden of Gethsemane He prayed, "My prayer is not that you take them out of the world but that you protect them from the evil one" (John 17:15).

His prayer contrasts with the direction of Christianity in the modern world. For the sake of their own protection, many Christians are evacuating the world. Our personal safety has taken precedence over our mission. The emergence of a separate-from-the-world Christian mentality is nullifying the need of Jesus' prayer. Why do we need to be protected from something we no longer encounter?

In contrast, it is clearly implied by His prayer that Jesus wants us to be in the middle of things, just as He was. He wants us to be vulnerable to the attacks of the world, out where His prayer is not just a nice idea from a morning devotional hour but a matter of survival. If we aren't out where it's dangerous, we mock Jesus' concern for our protection and undermine His reason for sending us as His ambassadors to the world.

Jesus never promised that our lives would be lived in peace; He promised that in the midst of this tumultuous, evil world, He would be our peace. There's a world of difference between those two perspectives.

Where's the graffiti? I'm sure that Jesus is quite familiar with the words written on the subway walls and tenement halls of our cities. And I wouldn't be surprised if He has even written something there for us all to read.

FEAR OF DANCING

*T*he Spirit of God dances. He can't be tamed. He won't be contained. He refuses to be confined to a weekend retreat, an evening meeting, or even a moment of devotion. He doesn't follow schedules, programs, or agendas, and He doesn't wait for His name to be called.

The Spirit of God dances. He dances right under the noses of those who don't believe in dancing; and He dances right on by those who do. He dances through the assemblies of the keepers of the dance, and right on out the door—and no one sees Him go.

And as the dancers continue the empty steps of their pantomime, the Spirit of God dances on out into the streets. He dances by the harlots in the red-light districts, by the victims of AIDS in lonely homes, by bag ladies in the inner cities, and by struggling farm families across the plains. He finds the orphans and widows and dances through the lonely pain of their lives. He dances through the camps of hungry children, through the crowded streets of the oppressed, and past the wire where the South African woman is hanging out ragged laundry as well as by the scrubbed white faces sitting in church in the nearby city.

Sometimes the dance turns to mourning, but always there's the dance. Happy dance or sad dance . . . the Spirit of God always dances.

His favorite dancing places are those where the keepers of the dance don't want Him to go: on MTV, on drive-in movie screens, or on smoky stages with microphones that smell of whiskey. The Spirit of God loves sinners and dances best where life spills out on the floor.

Occasionally He dances on the clean, sweet-smelling stages of the keepers of the dance—but not as often as He would like. He dances there when the keepers need Him: when there is pain, whenever life spills out on the floor. But usually the floor is clean and the dance is simulated, carefully choreographed by the keepers of the dance to use only those steps with which they feel secure.

The Spirit of God refuses to be choreographed. His dance is raw, new, and jerky. It's not always pleasing to the eye, but His dance is fresh in the lives of human beings whose floors have not been cleaned up. It isn't well-rehearsed, polished, or perfect; it slips and slides, sometimes innovative and shocking and at other times just exhilarant, but it's always real.

Most people, even those who pride themselves in their dancing, are afraid of this spontaneous dance. They're afraid of anything they can't control; and His dance is wild, unmanageable, even mad. But most important, it's vulnerable, open to criticism—the quality they fear most. So they must create their own dance of predictable steps and prescribed routines and send all their people through dance school—or outlaw dance all together.

But this should come as no surprise. It has always been this way. The Lord of the Dance himself was here once, and it was the same way then. He danced on the keepers' holy days and broke their holy laws. His timing—if not His whole dance—always seemed offbeat. He turned the tables on their dance in the Temple as He led a solemn dance of respect through their lighthearted nonchalance. He rode along Palm Drive atop a donkey at the head of the greatest hosanna dance ever.

He wanted to turn their empty religious movements into heartfelt, joyous dancing. He wanted them to exchange the grip

124

of the Law for the freedom of the dance. But they thought He was a clumsy dancer, always bumping into their traditions and stepping on their pious toes. He even danced with the wrong crowd, in smokefilled rooms and on messy floors.

Once He described His generation and declared, "We played the flute for you, but you would not dance; we sang a dirge, and you did not mourn. For John came neither eating nor drinking, and they say, 'He has a demon.' The Son of Man came eating and drinking, and they say, 'Here is a glutton and drunkard, a friend of tax collectors and sinners.' "

No, nothing's really changed . . . but the Spirit of God dances on.

UP ON THE ROOF

*T*he return of Christ has been covered from seemingly every angle in Christianity: from victorious promises of the King's triumphant return to assuring reminders that we all will go with Him. There are humorous anecdotes about the Rapture and even a song to leave behind for all those who will wish they'd been ready. We've covered every angle except one; and sadly, this one is the most important.

Every time the Second Coming is mentioned in the New Testament, it is brought up to encourage us to live *now* with greater intensity. Peter asks after reminding us of the coming of the Lord, "What kind of people ought you to be? You ought to live holy and godly lives" (2 Pet. 3:11). After teaching on the Rapture Paul concludes, "So then, let us not be like others who are asleep, but let us be alert and self-controlled" (1 Thess. 5:6). Christ concludes His own teaching on the subject by saying, "Who then is the faithful and wise servant, whom the master has put in charge of the servants in his household to give them their food at the proper time? It will be good for that servant whose master finds him doing so when he returns" (Matt. 24:45–46).

Even the Book of Revelation, whose major theme is the return of Christ, begins with a strong warning against spiritual mediocrity in this present age.

Biblical teaching on the Second Coming is always given for a reason—to wake us up to the reality of life here and now. The time is short; we have much to do. Let's get on with it.

But sadly, contemporary Christian culture is singing another tune in relationship to the coming of Christ. The song that exemplifies the current mood better than any other is not even a "Christian" song; it's a "moldy-oldy" first recorded by the Drifters in 1963: "When this old world starts to gettin' me down . . . I know a place that's trouble proof . . . up on the roof."

What a fitting theme song for our born-again culture to which the Second Coming has become no more than a way out. It's as if a whole society has taken up residence on the roof, far away from the noise and filth of the streets below, and is presently waiting for the holy helicopter to come and take it home where it belongs.

Our rooftop correspondent declares, "Yes, we're playing Christian music, doing Christian aerobics, and having a great time up here! All the prophetic indications tell us it could be any moment now, so check your rapture watches and stay tuned to Christian TV for the latest update!"

Twinkle, twinkle, coming Christ,
Take us all to paradise.

Escapism—that's the real danger. Escapism is a predominant theme in our culture in general today. Video games, TV, stereo "Walkmans," rock 'n' roll, sports, alcohol and drugs all attest to that. In many ways, preoccupation with the Second Coming has become simply one more means of avoiding reality.

But God always thrusts us *into* reality and responsibility by faith. He wants to stretch us, to bring us to maturity. His Church is His bride, but she is not ready for the wedding. She is not complete. It's a classic question of who's waiting for whom? We're sitting around waiting for the Bridegroom to show up while He's waiting for us to grow up.

But there is another reason why God is waiting. "The Lord is not slow in keeping his promise [to return], as some understand slowness. He is patient with you, not wanting anyone to perish, but everyone to come to repentance. . . . Bear in mind that our Lord's patience means salvation" (2 Pet. 3:9, 15).

Every day that the Lord tarries means more people are able to be saved. How selfish of us to want Him to close the door once we're in! Noah didn't go on board, shut the door, and wait for the rain. He was earnestly preaching a message of salvation right up until the first heavy drops of rain fell from a judgment-laden sky.

Even some people making missionary appeals have the audacity to motivate Christians to go to the mission field because Christ is not going to return until the Gospel has been preached to every nation. There are groups right now calculating which nations are left and are hard at work getting people to those nations who haven't heard so Christ can hurry back. The American Christian Church is pumping large sums of money into the nation of Israel under the presumption that it will fulfill prophecy and speed Christ's return.

This attitude translates to: "Okay, you guys, we want you to sit down and pay attention to the Gospel. We don't really care what you do with it (nor do we care about your physical condition, which, by the way, looks pretty bad right now); we just need to fulfill our obligation to preach the Gospel to every nation so that Christ can come get us out of here. Did everybody hear? Good. . . . Now, how many does that leave us, Joe? Hurry, the helicopter is waiting to take us back to the roof."

It's actually very simple. Our task, like Noah's, is twofold: to build the ark (to grow up together into maturity in the body of Christ), and to encourage everyone to come into that ark and be saved. It occurs to me that if Christ isn't in a hurry to get here, maybe we shouldn't be in such a hurry to leave.

Come on, let's get back down on the street where we belong!

ONLY ONE WORLD

*I*t's taken me a long time, but I think I'm starting to get it. I live in one world.

One world; an ugly one filled with war, disease, terrorism, rape, exploitation, hunger—I could fill the page—but that *is* the world. I have read my Bible from cover to cover, and I have not found any mention of another one. In fact, the world I find in the Bible seems to be basically the same as the one I live in.

The glorious news of the Gospel, of course, is that God came into this world in human flesh. He came in the person of His only begotten Son, Jesus Christ. Jesus did not come to create a little world within a world; He came straight from His Father in heaven to bring love, mercy, healing, and forgiveness into *this* world.

To do that, He lived in this world—you know, the ugly one, the only one we have, the one full of prostitutes, criminals, soldiers, lepers, and crazy maniacs. He lived in a world of people with wild eyes and smelly bandages, people who, if they moved in next door, would definitely bring down the property values.

The world Jesus came into is the same world He sends us

into as His followers. He prayed, "My prayer is not that you take them out of the world but that you protect them from the evil one. They are not of the world, even as I am not of it. Sanctify them by the truth; your word is truth. As you sent me into the world, I have sent them into the world" (John 17:15–18).

But instead of going into the world as we have been sent, we have created our own little world within a world. It's a world where "Christian" things are true, where everyone lives happily ever after, and, most importantly, where we can be safe from the "other" world—that big, scary one out there. Furthermore, the safety and security we count on so much in our own little world have less to do with Jesus Christ than with locks, fences, money, and the "right" neighborhood.

It's important to note that the born-again culture has been born and bred in this sheltered world-within-a-world, and that's why it finds itself so limited and so out of touch with the people Christ came to save. We have done just what He told us not to do. We have put our light under the bushel of a safe Christian subculture.

But the most distressing problem with this little world we have created is that, through it, we plan to escape the ugliness of the other world. We are glad to be insulated and prefer to watch Christian news, listen to Christian music, and have only Christian friends. We get more excited about the number of Christians who are in our office than we do about the number of non-Christians who are there for us to love. The truth is, we don't love non-Christians; we don't even like them. They swear, they have different values, and they wear smelly bandages.

We like our little world. We feel safe here. But our little world is a fantasy. If you look hard enough, you'll find as many crimes here as you do in the real world; they're just more carefully concealed. The safety of this little fantasy world is a fantasy, too. Why? Because we really live in only one world, and it's an ugly one.

Sooner or later that world is going to come crashing in on our little fantasy world-within-the-world. Sooner or later the rapist is going to break into our house, the riot is going to spill over into our street, or the bomb is going to go off under our car. It's inevitable. There's no way to escape the danger of life in this hostile world because, after all, the world *is* our address.

We have to get beyond being shocked and horrified by what we see in the world and get on with walking into it with the love and mercy of Jesus Christ.

When we do, we will finally realize that safety has nothing to do with locks, that security has nothing to do with fences, that joy has nothing to do with the absence of pain, and that peace has nothing to do with comfort. We will no longer confuse the securities of our subculture with the presence of Christ.

We will know the real Christ sustaining us in the real world, where He once sustained himself by doing the will of His Father. We will also hurt with the world, bleed for it, and cry over it just as Jesus did. We will be in danger and touch the unclean bandages.

The question is simple and straightforward: Are you in the world or are you escaping it? The issue is black and white. You are either walking into the world and into reality or you are walking away from it and into fantasy—because there's only one world and it's an ugly one.

THE IN'S AND OUT'S OF IT

In it, not of it," the statement was made
As Christian One faced the world, much afraid.
"In it, not of it," the call was made clear,
But Christian One got something stuck in his ear.
"Not in it, or of it" was the thing that he heard.
And knowing the world was painfully absurd,
He welcomed the safety of pious retreat,
And went to the potluck for something to eat.

Now Christian Two, he knew what to do,
He'd show those fundies a thing or two!
How will the world ever give Christ a try
If we don't get in there and identify?
So "In it, and of it," he said in his car,
As he pulled in and stopped at a popular bar.
"I'll tell them the truth as soon as I'm able
To get myself out from under this table."

Now along comes Christian Three jogging for Jesus,
In witnessing sweats made of four matching pieces.

His earphones are playing a hot Christian tune
About how the Lord is coming back soon.
"Not in it, but of it," he turns down the hill
And stops in for a bite at the Agape Grill.
Like the gold on the chain of his "God Loves You" bracelet,
He can have the world without having to face it.

While way up in heaven they lament these conditions
That come from changing a few prepositions.
"Not in it, or of it," Christian One thought.
But who in the world will know that he's not?
"In it, and of it," thought Christian Two.
But who in the world will know that he knew?
"Not in it, but of it," thought Christian Three.
But who in the world watches Christian TV?

And Jesus turns to Gabriel, shaking His head.
" 'In it, not of it,' wasn't that what I said?"

MESSENGERS IN DISGUISE

*T*here once was a kind Everlasting King who ruled a vast empire of mortals. This king kept many things about himself hidden from his subjects because these things were far too wonderful for mere mortals to comprehend. Nevertheless, he treated his people well because he loved them and wanted the best for them.

But they were ignorant people. Some were evil, smarter than the others, who spread bad rumors about the king. The people believed these rumors and revolted against the king, sending him into hiding.

For hundreds of years after, generation after generation set up mortal kings who ruled wickedly and made life miserable for them. But the evil ones kept convincing the people that they were better off with their own king than under the thumb of the all-powerful Everlasting King.

Meanwhile, the Everlasting King sent secret messengers from his palace (for he always did things in disguise) to remind the people of who he was and how good things had been for them when he was ruling. The messengers sang and danced the wonders of the king. A few people believed, but most did not and elected to put the messengers to death or send them into exile.

Finally, the Everlasting King sent his own Everlasting Son in disguise. For three years his son roamed the kingdom singing and dancing and reminding the people of the love and kindness of his father. Alas, the people didn't even listen to him; they put him to death as they had so many of the others.

. . . At least they thought they had. Of course, they couldn't kill him because he was everlasting. But he let them think they had—all except a few who truly believed he was the Everlasting Son of the Everlasting King.

These followers were secretly empowered by the king to spread the news of the Everlasting Son of the Everlasting King to all lands and for all generations. Because of this, these people and all who believed through them were called *Kingsons*.

For centuries Kingsons were treated by the people just like the Everlasting Son and his messengers had been. The Kingsons were stoned, sawed in two, and put to death by the sword. They went about in sheepskins and goatskins, destitute, persecuted, and misunderstood. The kingdom was not worthy of them.

But the Kingsons went on singing and dancing their message, receiving their persecution with joy because the Everlasting Son had told them to expect this. He said they would be hated just like he had been hated. And so they were proud to share in his sufferings.

But then a very wonderful thing happened (or so it seemed for a while). For some unperceived reason, the persecution ceased. Whether the heart of the people softened or the Kingsons were no longer found to be a threat, no one knew for sure, but Kingsons everywhere suddenly found themselves free to sing and dance at will. They banded together and sang and danced their message across the land. Soon they developed their own small kingdom of followers of the son of the Everlasting King. It wasn't long before every cultural expression in the evil kingdom had an equivalent Kingson expression in the Kingson kingdom.

For a while, the Kingsons basked in their freedom. Kingson messengers sang and danced for Kingsons. Everyone rejoiced, even the evil kingdom, because the Kingsons were so busy singing and dancing for each other, they didn't bother the evil kingdom anymore.

But something began to sour. The Kingsons grew tired of hearing the same message. And the Kingson messengers grew tired of singing and dancing the same message before the same people who, they soon realized, were growing tired of the same message. As they grew tired of the message, the messengers began to bicker about how the message was to be delivered.

And as the sound of the message grew old in the ears of the Kingsons, their love for the Everlasting King grew old as well. They liked living in a private kingdom where Kingson things surrounded them, but they lost their zeal for the king. What's more, there arose even among the Kingsons evil men, smarter than the others, who used Kingson words and truths to advance their own power and glory. Ultimately, maintaining a comfortable, secure Kingson kingdom became more important to Kingsons than the words and message of the king's son himself.

So it remains until this day. The Everlasting King looks out from his concealed palace and sighs with sadness. Once again, he sends secret messengers into his vast kingdom (for he always does things in disguise).

But he finds his messengers are better received in the old, evil kingdom than in the Kingson kingdom. For in the old kingdom, the people have been so long without kindness and love that many are finally willing to listen. Meanwhile, the Kingsons think they know all about the message as well as exactly how it should and should not be delivered.

And once again, the king's messengers are misunderstood and persecuted everywhere. But then, that's just the way the Everlasting Son said it would always be.

TORCHLIGHTS

An Open Letter to the Kingson Singers and Dancers

I just heard about a wave of shake-ups in the ranks of Christian music: top record company personnel resigning without notice, artists firing managers, record companies firing artists, and major tours losing big bucks. These events once again call into question the future of Christian music. Are its days numbered?

I'd like to suggest that apart from the personal pain to individuals involved, a shake-up in Christian music is probably a good thing. I'll go one step further: unless there's some kind of change, Christian music is headed for either oblivion or the meaningless repetition of proven formulas in a subculture that no longer matters to the world—which is pretty much the same as oblivion.

In many ways, Christian music to date could be described as a *novelty*. Putting spiritual words and principles into contemporary music was a great idea—a novel thing to do. When a person first realizes that something like this exists, it can be a truly exciting thing. But a person can't feed off that excitement for very long. "Wow, we've got music just like them!" will last for about a year at best. Sooner or later we've got to give people more.

Furthermore, although Christian music has been in existence for more than fifteen years, the audience has remained relatively young. Where are all those people who grew up with Christian music? Could it be that they outgrew it? That once the novelty wore off, there wasn't enough substance to hold them?

Throughout history, artists have been the most influential leaders of a culture. The anti-war, love, and peace movements of the sixties were almost single-handedly inspired by musicians. Their songs led marches as they lit fires of passion across the nation.

Today in Central America, the musicians, film makers, and poets give voice to the helpless cries of the common people— the peasants being crushed beneath the world's political machines. It's the artist who can reach the heart and stir the spirit to act.

But what about the Christian community in America today? Where have we, as Christian artists, brought Christians in sixteen years?

Well, we've told them in a thousand different ways that God loves them, and they liked that. We've told them to praise God, and they've done that. We've told them they were in a battle, but not to worry because they'll win in the end; and they liked that. And we've told them over and over again that soon the King is going to come and punish the bad guys and take the good guys to be with Him forever. And they liked that best of all.

But how many ways can we say these things? And how many times can our audiences hear it until they grow hard of hearing and bored? That's only the first of the questions which comes to mind as I think back over these last sixteen years.

Did we tell them of their responsibility to love their neighbor? Did we represent to them the lonely hearts of the people who surround them every day? Did we stir in them a compassion for the sick, the hungry, the homeless, the prisoners—pictures that artists know how to paint?

And were we honest with them about our own lives? When we went through great pain, did we take them with us? Did we share our unanswered questions with them? Did we force them

138

to face their own lives by forcing them to face ours?

Did we bring our doubts out into the open so they wouldn't feel so alone in theirs? Did we write about our failures and the things they taught us? Did we paint common, everyday pictures of loving God and loving each other? Did we paint such a clear picture of our own sins that it nearly scared us—and them—to death?

Did we sing to them of the dangers of spiritual pride, bigotry, and racism? Did we stimulate our fellow Christians to recognize truth wherever they found it, even when it was growing and flowering in a secular field?

Did we use the power of music to take Americans beyond the complacent confines of Western culture and awaken them to the needs of the world beyond—the Third World? Did we give them a feeling of what real suffering is? Did we stir them to action? Did we ignite fires in their souls?

Artists have always carried the torches that light the spiritual fires in a culture. I have one, and so do many of you. And it may not be too late.

THE ART OF FROMMING

*F*or many, *fromming* is the reason why we have Christian schools, Christian movies, Christian nightclubs, Christian music, Christian aerobics, Christian TV. In fact, seemingly every aspect of popular culture and contemporary life sooner or later sprouts a Christian counterpart. *Fromming* has become the major justification for the Christian subculture now firmly rooted in contemporary society. It is also a convenient excuse for any shortcomings the "Christian" version displays when compared to its "secular" counterpart and when such a venture comes up short of funds.

From. It has become an all-important word in the apologetic rhetoric of popular Christianity. We are constantly being bombarded with *fromism*—*From* this, that, and the other thing, *From* all of the things we are being saved *from*. We are *frommed* in books, music, and from the pulpit.

For example, Christian television protects concerned viewers *from* the evils of sex and violence on network television and a host of movie channels. Christian nightclubs provide teenagers and singles with a healthy atmosphere in which to pursue relationships safely away *from* the sexual safaris of teen clubs and singles' bars. Christian aerobics allow a Christian weightwatcher to fight flab without having to fight off Tina Turner's sensual rasp at the same time. Christian schools enable parents to send their children into a classroom free *from* the godless monster of secular humanism and the jaws of Darwinian evolution. Contemporary Christian music allows hip Christians to roll without straying *from* the Rock. Christian videos provide wholesome entertainment safe *from* vulgar language, *from* vulgar living, and *from* a vulgar world.

It's not hard to see why *fromming* has become so popular. There's an awful lot of downright evil, horrible, dirty, and unsafe things in the world. The art of *fromming* develops the basic justification to *from* into reactionary thinking, negative fixation, fear motivation, and the avoidance of a higher calling.

Fromming has been one of the least desirable marks of Christianity for as long as I can remember; Christians are identified not so much for what they do but for what they don't do. When our only distinctiveness in society comes *from* avoiding certain things, we can easily fix our gaze on the evil and view the rest of the world judgmentally. But this earns us a negative identity.

Let's face it, there's power in *fromming*. Have you ever noticed that it's easier to get people to march *against* something than to get them out *for* something? It's easier to point out a problem than it is to provide a solution. It's much simpler to condemn a pornographic magazine than it is to convey a positive, healthy attitude toward sex. It takes less effort to run away *from* the world than to be a positive answer in the middle of the world.

This is why *fromming* is so successful. Human nature feeds on it—as do a host of "Christian" ministries that owe their pump, power, and purse to the cash benefits of *fromming*.

But what a boring way to live! All these *froms* are so depressing. Just say "from" and think about the shape of your face. Say it several times—*from, from, from, from, from.* You can't even smile when you say it because *from* and *frown* are cut from the same mold. With all of the things we are being saved *from*, all the *frowning* is getting us nowhere.

Fromming is simply not enough. We can't stop at telling people what they are being saved *from*. They need a good dose of *to*—*to* excellence, *to* learning, *to* creativity, *to* exploration, *to* ex-

141

perimentation, *to* God, *to* risk, *to* love, *to* life! We are called *to* do all this in the world.

The world doesn't need Christian movies; it needs Christians making movies. The world doesn't need Christian music; it needs Christians making music. The purpose of Christians in the world is not to provide an alternative but to infuse it with the light and flavor of life in Christ. You just can't do that and *from* at the same time!

To be sure, there is a biblical *from*. The most well-known *from* is found in the Lord's Prayer: ". . . and lead us not into temptation, but deliver us *from* the evil one" (Matt. 6:13). We also find one in Jesus Christ's prayer for all the believers: "My prayer is not that you take them out of the world but that you protect them *from* the evil one" (John 17:15). In both cases the deliverance is not a deliverance *from* the world but a protection *from* evil and the evil one—preservation made necessary by our continued presence and involvement *in* the world.

Christ has not saved us *from* the world; He has saved us *to* the world. His prayer for all believers continues: "As you sent me into the world, I have sent them into the world" (John 17:18).

If we could just stop all this *fromming*, imagine what we could get down *to*!

HOLIER THAN WHO? OR HEAVEN CAN WAIT

*H*ave you ever been around a non-Christian who gets halfway into a juicy swear word, then falls all over himself when he remembers that you're a Christian?

Some Christians would be proud, thinking that their mere presence cleared the air a bit; but I don't like it. A situation like that always makes me feel detached from the human race, as if I just sprouted wings and wore this silly glow over my head. (Is this what Jesus meant by being a light in the world—glowing in the dark?)

Where do non-Christians get the idea that we're better than they are? I'm sure some of it comes from a sense of their own guilt, but I'm sure that we contribute to this "spiritual class system" by being dishonest about our own lives.

Christians get frustrated the same way other people do. We also worry about money, fight with our mates, lose our tempers, gossip, and distrust one another. We even swear; except we have "Christian" swear words like "gee," "darn it" and "shoot." Does changing a few letters somehow sanctify an outburst of anger?

It's true that spiritually we're seated with Christ in the heavenlies; but temporally we still have our feet firmly planted on earth, where our sanctification is still in progress. Heaven is our goal, but for now, heaven can wait.

It concerns me that non-Christians feel condemned by Christians. It concerns me to realize that some Christians are doing the condemning. If Jesus didn't come to condemn the world, why should we?

Jesus even earned the label "friend of sinners." This is truly remarkable when you consider that He was sinless. If anyone had the right to be "holier-than-thou," it was Christ; and if anyone should feel *condemned* around Him, it was sinners—especially sinners like prostitutes or crooked tax collectors. Yet these people found Him to be their friend: a strong affirmation of Christ's humility as the Son of Man.

A friend is someone who allows you to be yourself while encouraging you to change, so I doubt these people cleaned up their acts when Christ was around. Jesus must have endured some vulgar language for the sake of trying to get through to these people's hearts. They must have felt His love in spite of themselves.

Isaiah prophesied that the Christ would be "meek and lowly of heart." What a beautiful description of Jesus' compassionate attitude toward sinful people. His heart dredged the bottom of humanity; He knew it all; nothing could shock Him.

Our idea of righteousness, on the other hand, is much more fragile. It can easily be offended. I wonder if this is because our hearts aren't opened far enough to deal effectively with the sin in our own lives. We feel less guilty about tolerating our own comparatively "little" sinful compromises by vehemently condemning the gross sins of others.

It's time for Christians to rejoin the human race, to face our own humanity and find the ability to look compassionately on our other friends in the world. Our link with the world is our humanness. We don't have wings and we don't glow in the dark, but we do know who forgives us and gives us hope.

When Jesus began His ministry, He proclaimed the beginning of the acceptable day of the Lord. He accepted sinners on the basis of the Cross.

That day is still here and our purpose is to continue to proclaim it, not to delete expletives. Some Christians give us the impression that our purpose is to establish righteousness and judge sin. However, these are Christ's duties, and neither is His concern right now. Sin has already been judged on the Cross, and righteousness will be established in heaven.

But this is earth; heaven can wait but our neighbors can't. Let's be honest and let's be friends; through our humanity let's point people to our salvation . . . and theirs.

If all we do is make non-Christians feel we're better than they are, we've truly missed our mission in the world.

THEY ARE BLINDED

*S*ome people just don't get it. You can shine the light right in their faces and, like a deer frozen by approaching headlights, they never see a thing until it's too late.

It's a tragedy of this fallen world that people cannot see the light of the Gospel. It's not that they haven't been exposed; some have been overexposed. They stare at the light but they don't see it.

Have you ever been at a meeting where the Gospel was presented so clearly and convincingly that you wondered how anyone could go away without becoming a Christian? Or have you read a book like C. S. Lewis's *Mere Christianity* and thought if everybody could read that book, they would all be persuaded that the Gospel is true? It makes so much sense. Why don't they see it?

They have been blinded.

"And even if our gospel is veiled, it is veiled to those who are perishing. The god of this age has blinded the minds of unbelievers, so that they cannot see the light of the gospel of the glory of Christ, who is the image of God" (2 Cor. 4:3–4). The Gospel shines forth with light and glory, but they have no ability to see it!

For those seeking new and contemporary ways of presenting the truth to the world, this is an important and sobering reality. Important because we realize there is more at work than simple persuasion, sobering because it reminds us we are doing spiritual battle with an enemy more powerful than ourselves.

If we fail to understand this, we can fall into a number of blind traps ourselves.

1. We can go overboard trying to convince people of the Gospel. We may even alter it to make it more acceptable to worldly tastes.

2. We can rely on human methods such as emotional appeals, scare tactics, etc., to coerce people into Christianity.

3. We can become exasperated with people, start screaming at them or beating them with our Bibles. It's unnecessary. If they can't see a candle burning in the dark, they won't see approaching headlights either. They are blind and, as a friend of mine says, "You don't kick a blind man for running into a tree."

4. We may take their rejection personally. We may erroneously conclude that their lack of response is the result of our failure to persuade them. This sense of failure can even prompt us to use our own persuasive efforts with greater intensity. We scream louder and play the hymn through one more time.

All these problems stem from the assumption that we can make people see truth. We can't make people see; we can only make the Gospel clear. As Paul declared, "By setting forth the truth plainly we commend ourselves to every man's conscience in the sight of God" (2 Cor. 4:2).

As we do this, we must accept the reality that some people are blinded. We are in battle, but much of the warfare is beyond our sight. It's a spiritual battle in which God reveals and Satan blinds. Who sees and who doesn't is not our responsibility; our responsibility is only the clear, unadulterated presentation of the truth.

In that truth lies the hope that can even render Satan's veil powerless. As Paul goes on to declare, "For God, who said, 'Let light shine out of darkness,' made his light shine in our hearts to give us the light of the knowledge of the glory of God in the face of Christ" (2 Cor. 4:6).

147

Only God can make light shine out of darkness. Anyone else must have a lamp hidden in the darkness in order to pull off this trick. But God can create light where there is no light and where there is no source of light: light out of nothing, light *out of the darkness*.

This is the wonderful miracle. Satan may blind hearts, but God can bring light out of that darkness in men's hearts. He doesn't even need to penetrate Satan's veil. He is a God of miracles. He simply commands, "Let light shine out of darkness"— and there is light.

Our responsibility is summed up in Paul's simple but beautiful statement: "For we do not preach ourselves, but Jesus Christ as Lord, and ourselves as your servants for Jesus' sake" (2 Cor. 4:5). Jesus Christ himself is the light we hold out to the world, the steady, clear burning candle in the darkness to which people will be drawn as God gives them eyes to see.

May our light be this candle in the dark and not the headlights of onrushing traffic.

JESUS ("bleep")

I've been trying to ignore this for some time now, but I can't any longer; it just keeps coming up. Every time I type a chapter on this Smith Corona XE 5100 Spell-Right typewriter, I am faced with a dilemma: my typewriter bleeps.

I remember George Harrison's lament, "My guitar gently weeps," on the Beatles' famous white album. Well, my typewriter gently bleeps, or more accurately, "sickly" bleeps. It's a very pathetic, injured sound, like a little tone sort of bent over another. It reminds me of an ailing little lamb with half a vocal chord—not that I've ever been around an ailing little lamb with half a vocal chord, but I somehow think if I ever was it would sound like the bleep on my Smith Corona.

The bleep comes from a 50,000 word dictionary that has been programmed into the brains of this machine. Whenever I type a word that isn't on the list—"Bleebleep!"—it bleeps at me.

This is actually a very useful feature. More often than not, the bleep signals a typing error rather than a spelling mistake. But the spelling of particular words is an issue over which I and

149

the typewriter fight an ongoing controversy. Fifty thousand words is a lot, but not enough to get all the derivations of all the words I use, not to mention some words that have simply been programmed incorrectly or missed altogether.

So my typewriter has a bleep I cannot wholly trust, often sending me scurrying to my Webster's to defend myself. Imagine carrying on a running argument with your typewriter over the spelling of certain words.

But the real problem came when I began to suspect my typewriter was not a Christian. I first started to notice it on certain theological words like *sanctification, glorification, Christology,* and *soteriology* (which got bleeped twice).

Soon I discovered a very interesting thing when I typed the word *Christian*. It gets by unscathed, but *Christians* gets bleeped. Apparently my typewriter can handle one Christian at a time, but the idea of two or more of these things at once sends it squealing off like a sick lamb. This I-can-handle-one-but-don't-give-me-two phenomenon also applies to *Baptists, Presbyterians,* and *Fundamentalists.* Unfortunately for *Methodists,* they get bleeped before I can get to the final "t". I'm not even sure I want to mention what happens to *Pente*(bleep)*costal*(bleep)*s*(bleep).

But by far the biggest problem is the fact that my typewriter bleeps *Jesus.* Now it's true that many other common names get bleeped as well, but it's hard to understand how a typewriter that knows *John, Dick, Harry,* and *Sally* would not even know a name as important as *Jesus.* The final proof came when I found out *Buddha* got by without a sound!

I can't deny it any longer; I'm going to have to face the hard facts: I'm dealing with a pagan typewriter.

What shall I do? I'm trying to type out sanctified stuff and I'm getting bleeped all over the place! Well, as you can imagine, I've given this much thought and I've come up with three possible solutions.

1. Smash it. The thought that anything sanctified could ever come through a typewriter that gives Jesus the bleep is unthinkable. This typewriter shouldn't be allowed to live! Even if I sold it, I would be sending another pagan influence out into the world to corrupt someone else's mind. A typewriter that accepts Buddha and bleeps Jesus is certainly going to lend support to an already acceptable secularized world view. (Would you believe,

I just got bleeped on *secularized*?)

2. Surely someone out there in Christian World USA, some Christian electronic whiz-kid, has come up with a new mind for this thing. Perhaps I don't have to get rid of the whole typewriter, after all; I can just get it saved, take it to an electronic revival meeting. Someone must have thought of this by now.

3. I suppose I could find a way to use it as it is. I could use it as a reminder that I live in a world that is constantly bleeping Jesus. Every time I type that final *s* in His name and hear that sick squeal, I could feel the pain and reality of rejection. After all, "He came to his own and his own received him not."

Ah, but I cannot let myself off that easily. I cannot think myself more noble than the rest of this world for enduring a pagan Smith Corona; I am part of this bleeping world, too. The real truth I must face about all this bleeping is that I too bleep Jesus.

I bleep Him whenever I compromise my faith. I bleep Him when I'm lazy and refuse to do what He wants in a given situation, when I'm so caught up in myself I can't care for someone else, when I fail to see His hand moving in all that goes on around me, and when I go through life forgetting that He is the most important thing in my memory bank.

But realizing this doesn't merely leave me lamenting my bleeping self; it fills me with wonder to realize that He still uses my life. He goes on typing His truth right through all my bleeps into the reality of my life and the people I touch. I have to believe this or I will close my lid and be silent forever because I know that I am not a perfect instrument.

I think I'm going to keep this typewriter just as it is. After all, God has not smashed me or traded me in for another model. The fact that I can sanctify this typewriter through the truth of the words that pass through it, in spite of its bleeps, reminds me that God can do the same thing through my bleeping life in this bleeping world.

AN INSIDE JOB

*P*ornography controlled Brad. His walls were papered with suggestive posters and his magazine collection rivaled that of the local adult bookstore. When he became a Christian, he sought help for his problem. A friend's counsel was simple and direct: strip the walls and burn the magazines.

A week after the purge, Brad was talking with his friend again.

"Well, how's it going?" his friend asked.

"Terrible," Brad replied. "I did what you said, but now I stare at blank walls and see the most graphic pornography I've ever seen."

Brad's story illustrates the complex problem of trying to be pure in a polluted world. To clear Brad's room of all that unhealthy stimuli was certainly a step in the right direction, but to believe that it was enough to curb his appetite is to ignore the real problem of evil.

The cartoon character Pogo's famous statement says it best: "We have met the enemy and he is us." A pure environment doesn't necessarily make pure people. Avoiding movies, burning records, staying away from dances, or turning off the radio does not make anyone spiritually strong. In fact, these actually tend to produce the opposite effect, developing fragile Christians who must live in a controlled, censored environment—much like people who are so sensitive to germs and chemical pollution that they have to live in sterile rooms and breathe only filtered air.

The real problem of evil is inside us and not on our walls or our stereo turntables. The purifying process must begin in the heart and mind. The Bible says: "To the pure, all things are pure, but to those who are corrupted and do not believe, nothing is pure" (Titus 1:15). God works from the inside out, not outside in. A pure heart makes for a pure world, not vice versa.

A pure heart comes from knowing Jesus Christ and having Him recreate our hearts and minds through His Word. It's strictly an inside job. Once that process of change has begun, we begin to see differently. The Word of God becomes a compass that points us toward truth. With our new-found eyesight, we begin to sift out truth from wherever we find it—even in the most unlikely places. "To the pure, all things are pure."

Sacred and *secular* are not labels we attach to external things. The sacred/secular distinction is actually a matter of eyesight, and you always find what you're looking for.

For the Brad in all of us, the answer is not just a blank wall. The answer is to look into the Word and have our eyesight reconstructed. Then, as we walk through the world, we can see things correctly, rather than having to be victimized by it or protected from it.

GARBAGE IN, GARBAGE OUT?

*T*o remain pure in this worldly, impure environment, many Christians believe that they must screen what they see and hear. Contact with the secular world is to be avoided as much as possible. Spiritual authorities are called upon to act as moral environmental protection agencies, monitoring the air around their followers' eyes and ears, attempting to keep it free from evil pollutants.

The assumption is that people are what they read and become what they hear. Take in a good thing, you become better; take in a bad thing, you become worse. Introduce garbage into a person's mind and it ruins his character. In computer terms: it's known as, "garbage in, garbage out."

Paul tells us, "Whatever is true, whatever is noble, whatever is right, whatever is pure, whatever is lovely, whatever is admirable—if anything is excellent or praiseworthy—think about such things" (Phil. 4:8). To a degree, the "garbage in, garbage out" theory is true. However, this passage concerns the things we choose to hold in our minds—what we meditate on—not what we must touch, see, and hear while living in this world. It isn't

154

a command to become cultural ostriches.

Nevertheless, many have turned to a head-in-the-sand approach to Christian purity. They assume that if we hear no evil and see no evil, we will most certainly speak no evil.

This position is unrealistic for two reasons. First, it is built on a false assumption about the nature of evil. It's easy to put the focus of our battle for purity on keeping worldly garbage out and yet avoid hauling out the garbage that's already in. The prophet Jeremiah declares, "The heart is deceitful above all things and beyond cure" (Jer. 17:9). Jesus echoed that when He pointed out that it's not what goes into a man that defiles him, but what comes out (Matt. 15:11).

Struggling with evil exclusively on an external level often conceals our own sin, leading to self-righteous piety instead of real purity. Hiding from the garbage that's already in us keeps us from our point of contact with a fallen world. We lose our sense of compassion, become judgmental, and end up condemning the world rather than identifying with its fallenness and bringing it the good news of salvation as Jesus did.

The second reason why the head-in-the-sand approach to purity is unrealistic is that we will remain frustrated tempts to avoid worldliness, even if our battle with evil were solely external. A flick of the dial, a glance at a billboard, a walk by the newsstands, a look in the paper, a song on the radio, or any ordinary daily occurrence can bring us face to face with some unclean thing. Then what?

The important issue is not to keep the garbage out, but to deal with it, to pick through it, and to process it. This is where we must be careful.

If we don't process it, "garbage in, garbage out" will properly describe our lives. We can unwittingly be affected by what we see and hear if we become passive receivers. Do I sit glued to the TV without noticing whether lies or truth are presented as solutions to human problems? Do I sing along with songs on the radio without thinking about the words? Is my mind in gear, or neutralized through passive involvement?

The Bible asserts, "The spiritual man makes judgments about all things" (1 Cor. 2:15). It declares that a mature man discerns good from evil (Heb. 5:14) and that real purity isn't so much an external matter as it is internal: "To the pure, all things are pure" (Titus 1:15).

The spiritual man in an unspiritual world doesn't stand aloof, unsullied and unscathed, from humanity. He walks with compassion among men, learning to spot good and evil, truth and error—in himself and in his world.

A truly spiritual man participates in the world and actively listens, neither avoiding the garbage nor ignorantly accepting it. Sorting through life's rubble, he finds treasures. For, however fallen, this is still our Father's world.

 Christian in our at

45

MIND-WASTE

A mind is a terrible thing to waste." So goes the ad for the United Negro College Fund. It occurs to me there is more than one way to waste a mind. One way, alluded to in this advertisement, is to deprive it of information, keep it illiterate and ignorant.

Another more common but less obvious way to waste a mind is to fill it full of useless information, stuff that will keep it occupied endlessly with shallow concepts. If we fill it full of facts, trivia without any real value, we have wasted a mind.

Thirty years of television coming back at us all at once through sixty cable channels has opened the possibility of wasting a mind through trivia overload. Never in the course of human events have so many known so much about so little. Everyone seems to know what to buy, what to wear, what to see, and what to hear; but the deeper questions of who we are, why we're here, and where we're going have been buried under an avalanche of trivia.

Some of us have had the privilege of encountering a person with an exceptionally sharp mind. Perhaps it was a grandmother who read, a professor who challenged us to think, or a minister who made us go back through why we are a Christian, but these people are always exceptions to the rule. We are, by and large, a generation geared toward mental shortcuts.

Enter the computer. It can be argued that the computer is an amoral tool of man capable of good or evil, depending upon the hands into which it falls. It can also be argued that the computer is not a mere mindless machine bent on the ultimate takeover of the human race, but a tool programmed by human minds to make a myriad of resources readily available to the fingertips of the average man.

It can also be argued, however, that the computer is dangerous in that it makes the minds of a few accessible to many. In essence, fewer people are doing the thinking, but they make their ideas accessible to many people quickly.

But what happens to the time that we save by this process? If this mental convenience can set men free to think higher thoughts, then it has truly been of service, but if it merely programs man to receive an endless stream of mental junk, then we'd be better off going back to slide rules and multiplication tables.

And what about the lost art of reading? Libraries are fast becoming the relics of the twentieth-century. A flick of the switch has replaced the solitary turn of the page and drained the verdant forest of man's mind into a video vacuum.

What of conversation, that challenge of discovery and disclosure which allows us a look into the mirror of human relationships: into the desires, dreams, doubts and destinies of the human heart? What of the painful process of confrontation, where ideas are hammered out as iron sharpens iron? When do we have time for any of these anymore?

Instead, our twentieth-century lifestyle has left the switch on and the mind off, and there's no place to dump the truckloads of unsanitary mindfill that accumulate on the curbs of Brain Street.

In the middle of all this cultural mind-waste is the contemporary Christian who finds his mind is no less in jeopardy because of his faith. Not only must he fight the current of popular culture, but he must also pick his way through the garbage of false teaching that tells him to give up his mind for God. Listening to the average popular preacher gives the impression that the audience can't think. As the camera pans the rows of faces, the audience gives the impression they fully agree with him. Their appearance is fairly predictable: "My mind is open; pour it in."

The Scriptures discourage this intellectual passivity. In the Book of Acts, the Bereans were commended because they received Paul's message with great eagerness and "examined the Scriptures every day to see if what Paul said was true" (Acts 17:11).

The Bible calls us to the renewal of our minds, to be nourished with truth and sharpened like a sword for battle. God is not asking us to turn our brains to mush for His sake, to mindlessly obey and blindly accept what someone else calls truth.

God wants us to use our minds, to test the spirits, to discern good from evil, to study to show ourselves capable of handling the Word of God correctly, and He wants us to hold on to faith and a good conscience. He wants mindful obedience, participation. He is not seeking a relationship with robots who spit out programmed truth on demand without the integrity of their own choice to follow that truth.

At the bottom line is the issue of integrity. Am I a co-participant with God or am I a spiritual clone? Do I sign my mind over on the dotted line or do I bring it before God each day ready to question, to test, and to choose that which is being revealed to me through the Spirit?

This is the challenge, and it is a heady one indeed for the contemporary Christian who must fight the battle of the mind on two fronts. On the cultural front, one must struggle to keep the mind from being wasted by senseless overload. Meanwhile, on the Christian front, one must keep the mind from being wasted by false teaching that equates mindless passivity and obedience while critical thinking is considered rebellion.

It's not easy, but then again, a mind, created and given by God, is a terrible thing to waste.

Thou shalt love the Lord thy God with all thy . . . mind.

HUEY'S LADDER

*A*s I write this chapter, Huey Lewis and the News hold the number one hit single in the country: "Jacob's Ladder," written by Bruce Hornsby. (By the time you read this, it will be history, but that's pop music.) The chorus goes:

Step by step
One by one
Higher and higher
Step by step
Rung by rung
Climbing Jacob's ladder.

It sounds good, has a great guitar part, energetic beat, and makes me want to start climbing.

It also reminds me of the little chorus we used to sing in Sunday school:

We are climbing Jacob's ladder,
We are climbing Jacob's ladder,

We are climbing Jacob's ladder—
Soldiers of the cross.

Christians should get pretty excited about this biblical image becoming a number one hit. I can see it now, the next Christian magazine to hit my doorstep will boldly proclaim: "Jacob's Ladder Climbs to the Top of the Charts!"

But hold it. What *is* Jacob's ladder all about? Why are we on it and where are we going? Give Huey some credit; he takes this thing further than we ever did in Sunday school.

He tells us there's a fat preacher trying to sell him salvation, warning him about doom and gloom and asking for money to join his little band of saints. Huey doesn't want to be like the fat preacher and I don't blame him. I wouldn't either. But then he tells us instead that he doesn't need salvation; he's doing the best he can climbing up Jacob's ladder rung by rung. After all, he's "just another fallen angel trying to get through the night."

Oh-oh. What's this about being a fallen angel? And what's the ladder all about? Sounds like it's Huey's salvation. I wonder if this was what Jacob had in mind.

So I go back to the Sunday school version. Maybe it will shed some light on the subject. But sorry, no help here:

We are climbing Jacob's ladder,
We are climbing Jacob's ladder,
We are climbing Jacob's ladder . . .
Soldiers of the cross.

Oh great! What on earth does being a soldier of the cross have to do with climbing a ladder? Who wrote this thing anyway and why didn't anyone tell me what it meant?

Thoroughly bemuddled, I get out my Bible and look up the Genesis (not the rock group) account and find out there were indeed angels on that ladder, but they weren't fallen. They were God's angels passing up and down on the ladder as God, who was standing above it, spoke promises to Jacob about being the father of a great nation, continuing the promise given to his father Isaac and his grandfather Abraham.

So! There weren't any people on the ladder at all. Never were. The ladder was for God's angels carrying out His work in the world.

161

Suddenly I realized there's something wrong with both songs. What are Huey Lewis, Bruce Hornsby, you or I, or our children doing on this ladder in the first place? According to Jacob's dream, none of us belong there.

Suddenly I have a comic picture of God yelling down at us from the top, "Come on, you guys. Didn't you read the sign? 'Angels Only.' And what's with all the soldier getups? There's no battle up here. The battle's down there where you're supposed to be. Now get off this thing before I shake you all off!"

The truth of the matter is, not one person is working his way up any ladder to God. Salvation is the only way for us to get there. The fat preacher was right but he's doing it in the wrong way (and it wouldn't hurt if he lost some weight, too). So why am I taking you through this whole process, anyway? To prove that you and I as Christians in the world have got to be awake and alert. That alertness is just as necessary in the church as it is outside of it.

Truth and error are everywhere, but they're not going to pop up with labels attached. They have to be pursued, discovered, measured, and argued over just as I have done with this song.

We are in an age that makes it is easy to let culture or even Christianity wash over us. Jacob's ladder wasn't what Huey Lewis thinks it was, but it wasn't what my Sunday-school teacher thought it was either.

It took the Word of God to square this thing away, and it's the Word of God that will enable us to cut below the surface of anything deep enough to get at what it means. In fact, the Word is a double-edged sword that "penetrates even to dividing soul and spirit, joints and marrow; it judges the thoughts and attitudes of the heart" (Heb. 4:12). Every Christian possesses this penetrating sword and can cut deep into the heart of any matter to discern truth, but I fear most of us are stirring our gospel tea with it.

Soldiers of the cross on ladders? No. It's time to get back on the ground where we were first placed. Ladders are for angels.

"Oh, was that your hand I stepped on, Huey? I'm sorry. It's just that it's harder to get down off these things than it is to get up."

ONE HOUR OF MTV

*T*here is something different about this present generation of teenagers and I've been trying to figure it out. I used to think I could relate to them by remembering what things were like when I was in high school. No longer. These kids are living in a different world, coming from a place that I never knew existed.

It's not necessary to be a sociologist to realize this. Popular music has always been a fairly accurate test of a generation's values. Now, with the aid of music video, we can get a cultural reading very quickly.

One hour of MTV can teach us a lot about our teenage generation.

The first thing I notice is the absence of a generation gap mentality. There's nothing unusual about seeing musicians over forty playing alongside teenagers. Paul McCartney sings with Michael Jackson. Elton John is "still standing." Cyndi Lauper's parents appear in two of her videos and her mother is treated with touching love and respect in "Time after Time." Thomas Dolby's father plays a major role in "Hyperactive."

Believe me, things have changed. Can you imagine Crosby, Stills, Nash & Young in 1972 on the front lawn, surrounded by their smiling moms and dads?

The second thing I notice is the absence of "cool." You can be anything you want and still be accepted. Bobby-sox fifties, hippie-radical sixties, cool-down seventies, punk, square, leather, three-piece-suit businessman, or even Christian are all in. It doesn't matter; anything goes—as long as it hits the senses and makes some kind of impact.

That leads to the third, and what I feel is the most important, observation of youth culture today: For all intents and purposes, this is an *amoral* generation.

My generation grew up with a sense of right and wrong, good and evil. Our parents may not have remembered why they did it, but they held to the traditions with which they had been raised. However, it wasn't long before we discovered that those traditions were built on a traditional Christian faith that had eroded away. With the foundation gone, we found the building was a pushover.

Oddly enough, my generation is now rebuilding the very structures we destroyed—not out of any revival of faith, but merely out of the need for survival through the preservation of order and sanity. The social pendulum has swung far back to the right, but teenagers who grew up during its arc to and from the left are still feeling the consequences of that leftward swing. They were raised in a moral vacuum.

This is an essential insight for those who are communicating to youth today. According to many conservative evangelicals, today's youth are pitifully trapped in Satan's grip. Their approach to contemporary youth culture is to carry a rocket launcher and blow everything away.

But *amoral* isn't necessarily *immoral*. Evil is unquestionably present. An hour of MTV will most likely offer a self-glorifying, masochistic song by Billy Idol or the sexually violent Innuendos of Ratt. But that hour will also contain a positive celebration of life by Howard Jones or an inspiring encouragement to run the race and "you will surely cross the line" from Manfred Mann's Earth Band. There most certainly will be at least one statement an hour against the evils of war and, perhaps, a warning like "Don't pay the ferryman 'til he gets you to the other side" (Chris DeBurgh).

Let's face it: Satan not only has to fight God and the forces of light, but he also has to fight common sense as well. These kids are not dumb; in fact, some of them are figuring out a lot for themselves. Some have taken a long look at the gates of hell and decided they aren't interested.

I saw a video by Little Steven & the Disciples of Soul titled "Out of the Darkness." The looks on the musicians' faces told me they had seen enough. They were imploring everyone to reach out . . . take a hand . . . make a stand . . . come out of the darkness.

A surprising number of positive songs right now have a fresh, innocent appeal—almost as if the writers and singers had just discovered goodness. Perhaps they have . . . for themselves. There's definitely a new fascination with morality in our culture. We only have to read a few reviews of the *Star Wars* trilogy to get the impression that George Lucas invented good and evil. If this generation thinks he has, it's because young people haven't found it painted clearly anywhere else.

That's why we need to bring them the truth of Jesus Christ. They're ready and hungry, but we don't need rocket launchers. We don't need to be cool or beat around the bush. All these are unnecessary methods. Thank God! We can finally say goodbye to religious surveys, "I Found It!", campaigns, and youth group burger bashes.

Teenagers today are as open to those who carry the message of God as they are to the messengers of Satan. The only question is, who will reach them first?

DESPERATELY SEEKING LEAH

And these children that you spit on as they try to change their worlds are immune to your consultations. They're quite aware of what they're going through.

—David Bowie

This quote appears at the beginning of the movie *The Breakfast Club*. In the movie, five teenagers confined to their high school library for a Saturday of detention grapple with stereotypes, parents, and growing up. It's the first (and I think still the best) of a rash of movies released in the last few years that picture adolescents trying to cope in a threatening world.

All of them seemed to agree on one thing: teenagers are growing up in a virtually adult-free world where they are forced to figure out life for themselves without adequate role models or parental supervision. If there are parents at all, they're gone all the time, divorced and preoccupied with someone new, or so emotionally unstable that they need their kids to prop them up.

I used to wonder if this picture was very accurate until I struck up a conversation while sharing a hotel jacuzzi with a young teenager one night.

Her delicate features told me she was just a child, but her face betrayed a premature heaviness characteristic of the adult world. I threw out a couple questions to try to get over the uneasiness I felt being alone with her in a hot tub. I quickly found out David Bowie was right: she knew what she was going through.

In fact, she knew it so well she surprised me with how she could articulate her situation so clearly. Had I made up this conversation myself for a novel or a short story, I would have rejected it as being too well-developed for a person her age.

"Here for the weekend?" I asked.

"Yeah."

"Are you with a group?"

"No. I'm here with my parents, but they've abandoned me."

"What do you mean?"

"I might as well be living by myself. They're never home. My mom and dad both leave about 11:00 in the morning and get back about 3:00 the next morning. I never see them. When I do, we fight. I fight with my father mostly. It's no use. I've given up trying to be nice anymore. I usually let my father have it. He has it coming to him.

"He said he'd buy me a gun. A boy I know has threatened to rape me, so my father said he'd buy me a gun.

"Now, what am I supposed to do with a gun? I don't even know how to use one! Once I tried to run away to Canada but I didn't have enough money. I can't *wait* until I can make enough money to leave home. I might as well; I'm on my own now—it's just that I never got to be a kid."

"How old are you?"

"Sixteen."

"Do you ever tell your parents how you feel about all this?"

"Yeah."

"What happens?"

"They treat me like a baby for three days—bring me to a hotel like this—and then everything goes back to being the same."

"Why not tell your mom you want her home until you finish high school?"

"Oh no. I've gotten too used to not having them there. I don't think I could handle having my parents around now."

167

"How long has this been going on . . . your parents both gone so much?"

"About two years."

"Do you think if things could change and your parents were around more, you could be a normal 16-year-old?"

"No. It's too late. I don't think I'll ever have kids either."

Her cousin came and interrupted our conversation along with a hotel employee closing down the pool area. There was a brief exchange with two older boys in the game room; then she and her cousin were off down the hall toward their room. It occurred to me I hadn't gotten her name, but I had a feeling I knew what it was: *The New Teenager in America*. But for now, let's just call her Leah.

I wonder about Leah's generation.

Given the accessibility of birth control and the propensity each generation has toward avoiding the pitfalls of the former (getting married and having children, according to Leah's assessment of her parents' generation), I wonder if the new generation will have any children, if there will be any survivors.

One thing's for sure: love and caring are still the best ointment for healing a wounded society. The hardness that was already forming on Leah's 16-year-old face was simply a common defense against a lack of love. The saddest thing is, she's probably going to give herself away to somebody who will promise to give her in one night what she hasn't had for a lifetime.

I thought of the group of high school-aged young people I was with for the weekend. They were almost all Christians, here to attend a leadership conference at a Bible college. I found myself seeking Leah to bring her to our meeting the next morning. She probably would have found the games corny and some of the young people "uncool," but if she would have resisted at all, it would only have been on the surface. Deep down inside she would be longing to be part of a secure environment where she could truly be 16 again.

I thought of relatively healthy Christian families and the incredible ministry they could have by simply opening their doors—surrogate families to a whole neighborhood of wandering teenagers, homeless in their own sort of way.

Some of you who read this book can provide a home to the Leahs in your neighborhood. Teenagers are always going to their friends' homes when their parents are gone, so why not invite them to your house. It will probably mean putting up with some loud music, weird characters, and rearranged furniture. But a home that provides genuine acceptance, love, and caring will truly be what Jesus said we are to be: a city on a hill that cannot be hid.

I can't get to Leah, but I can get to you. Who knows? Maybe somewhere out there, one of you will find her before it's too late.

TRUTH, MICK JAGGER, AND PAINT BRUSHES

A teacher I highly respect once told me to affirm truth wherever I find it. It's advice that has served me well for many years. Like putting on a pair of glasses that filters out certain rays while letting others through, this approach to the world turns every encounter into a possible learning experience. Unlike the bifocals of a sacred/secular dualism, these glasses turn all events in life into spiritual experiences.

Jesus put truth in its purest, simplest form when He said, "I am the way and the truth and the life" (John 14:6). This is very important because it identifies truth with the person of Christ. Jesus doesn't merely point the way to truth; He *is* truth. He embodies truth, and all truth finds its beginning and ending, its Alpha and Omega, in the person of Jesus Christ. To know Him is to know truth.

Does that mean that the converse is also true: to know truth is to know Christ? I believe it does, although it is possible to encounter Him and not be aware of it.

It's like this. We all have our jigsaw puzzle called *Truth.* It has a million pieces and will never be completed in one lifetime.

Volumes of books have been written and countless schools founded for the purposes of explaining the puzzle, teaching various theories of how to put it together, and speculating over what the puzzle will look like if it is ever completed.

But an amazing thing happens when we accept Jesus Christ: we receive the box the puzzle came in. On the cover, as always, the completed puzzle is pictured, and it shows Jesus himself.

Knowing Who the puzzle is, however, doesn't absolve the Christian of the task of putting it together—this is still our life experience—but it does mean that each new discovery, each new piece we fit, gives a more complete understanding and experience of Jesus Christ our Lord. To encounter truth is to encounter more of Christ.

Unbelievers, too, can put pieces together; they just aren't sure what they are handling. It could be a section of hair, an edge of a fingernail, or the fringe of a garment. Someone might even come to the end of her life's work and be absolutely certain she has completed a nose, but whose nose? And how many other noses are there? And why is this nose so important?

Recently, Mick Jagger came out with a solo hit called "Let's Work." It really surprised me. Musically it sounded more like Bruce Springsteen than the raunchy Rolling Stones, and its content was a positive, motivational message on the value of work and the danger of laziness. The message of the song was truthful, and not only that, it was relevant to my needs.

I don't like work and will by nature avoid it if at all possible.

I marvel at my wife. She always works and seems to thrive on it. The only thing she doesn't like is getting up in the morning, but once she's up, there's no stopping her. Even when she quits working it's still dripping off her, like a nuclear power plant in meltdown.

I, on the other hand, have to drag myself to work. I have to work to work. Right now I am working very hard just to write this. Distracting me is easy and I can even think up creative distractions if I have to.

If I read my Old Testament, I find I am not alone. Work was Adam's curse, and because I bear his humanity and the seed of his sin, it is my curse as well. But because I also stand in Christ's salvation, I can find a redeeming of that curse in work—a fulfillment that even Adam may not have known.

Then along comes, of all people, the obnoxious, arrogant, pompous Mick Jagger encouraging me to redeem man's curse and warning me of what will happen if I don't. Hey, I don't know how he's done it—he may or may not know the picture on the cover of the box—but he has managed to put together a few pieces of the puzzle called *Truth*. He's joined the very pieces that I need to see right now, and I'll take it as truth.

If I were looking at the world through dualistic bifocals, I would have considered the source and immediately dismissed the possibility of anything good coming out of Nazareth, or even this station on the radio, for that matter, because it only plays "secular" music. I would also have to limit my spiritual experiences to those that happen in church on Sunday, with Christian friends, or through "anointed" ministries. But I definitely would have missed the spiritual experience I had listening to Mick Jagger admonish me to redeem the curse, while precariously straddling the desk and chair, holding a full gallon of paint, and stretching to reach the top edge of the molding without getting any paint on the ceiling.

TURNING OUT

(Author's Note: I'm going to let a group of college students con-clude this section on turning out into the world because they have said it better than I can. Their paper was a synopsis of a course I presented to a class of primarily youth ministry majors at a Chris-tian college. I also include part of the syllabus for the course to give the paper context. My thanks to all five of these students for their excellent insights.)

YM231 YOUTH IN CONTEMPORARY CULTURE

Instructor: John Fischer
Course Description and Objectives:

"What are you watching?"
"I don't know."
"What's it all about?"
"I don't know."
"Well, what's happening?"

"I think the guy in the black hat just did something terrible."

"What did he do?"

"You're so analytical! Sometimes you just have to sit back and let art wash over you."

—Conversation from the movie *The Big Chill*

It might be more accurate to say that the average American young person in this media-dominated age is more likely drowning in contemporary culture than that they are occasionally caught in its wave. Today's youth grow up plugged into the latest images. Their minds are on a direct-line hookup to the TV screen and the stereo headphones. What's going across that line, how it's understood by the teenager, and what the proper Christian response to it is are the themes of this course.

Jesus instructed Christians to be in the world but not of it. This position demands a discriminating awareness and yet, to date, the church's response to contemporary culture has been for the most part either reactionary (resulting in retreat) or nonexistent (resulting in unconscious involvement).

The purpose of this course is to develop a discriminating awareness of contemporary culture. To do this, we will explore three major areas of study:

1. Developing a theology of cultural awareness.
2. Interpreting popular art forms.
3. Developing a model of conscious Christian involvement.

CONSCIOUS INVOLVEMENT PAPER

Presented by: Glenn Fischer, Mary Moore, Dawn Johnson, Cindy Loux, John McKenna

The world is sleeping in the night
And the church just won't fight
'Cause we're asleep in the light.
How can we be so dead

When we've been so well fed?
Jesus rose from the grave
And we can't get out of bed.

—Keith Green*

We wait patiently for someone to take the initiative. Will it be God or us? We know perfectly well, as humans, our first tendencies are to stand silent and erect, glaring coarsely from behind the battle line. We are afraid of the wounded in the world, but more afraid of being wounded ourselves. We are afraid of reality and convinced by pride that darkness and light just don't mix. But at the same time, we easily imagine ourselves out in the world someday—exposing the darkness through God's light within us, even though it may be only a dim ray of our own insecurity.

As Christians, we are not so much aware of the world as we are aware of ourselves. We are obsessed at times with our spiritual standing more than with those who don't even have legs to stand on, never mind kneel in prayer. We serve ourselves with Bible studies and with morning, noon, and night church services while street people starve because no one is willing to serve them. Our religious convictions convict us, but we refuse to relate with the convicted behind bars.

Somewhere along the line our priorities have been distorted. We face the danger of secluding ourselves within the church and erasing any feelings of obligation to reach out to the world. We choose not to conform to society or its culture out of fears and insecurities in ourselves. But in choosing nonconformity, we create our own conformity: comfortable Christianity. It's our crutch in a time of need, while we're afraid of the blood, violence, and greed of the wilderness jungle—the real world. We use Christianity and abuse it too many times as a shelter from the pain and remorse.

So how do we cut through into the real world? What is that first step in becoming aware of the needs of our world (God's world) instead of ourselves? First, as Oswald Chambers points out in his book *My Utmost for His Highest*, we must realize that we cannot do what God does, and God will not do what we can do. We have to work out the salvation God has worked in.

Conscious involvement is a twofold enterprise. We not only have to be aware that God is at work in our lives, but we must work out that awareness in a world that is unaware of God's love, unaware of justice and reason, love and mercy, identity and heart.

We are called to awaken to the world around us, to seek Christ's direction and look at the world through His eyes instead of our own. We are to be obedient, to take the direction He gives us. We are to spread the same love to others that Christ has so freely given to us.

How we appear to our Christian brothers and sisters should not hinder our obedience to the call God has laid before us. We must not be afraid of what other Christians think of us when we are in the world. After all, Jesus had to deal with persecution. What we should be concerned with is what non-Christians see in us, for they will see right through us.

Bleeding hearts and images,
    aware of influence and rejection;
We choose reality, you see infection.
Split decisions, split directions.
Stripped of our identity, no longer immune to passion or
    pain;
We give you our hearts, you poison the strain.
Down comes our religion, drowning in the pouring rain.

—GF

Dance through the good times; dance through the bad. Dance as if this time was all that you had.

—John Fischer
from the song "Dance" on the album *Casual Crimes*

PART

IV

ROUND ABOUT

*T*he warm South African summer air filled the room with a mixture of body odors and fragrant smells from a room full of people all foreign to me, twisting my seasonal clock upside down here on the bottom of the world in December. It was the first annual Christian Artists Seminar at a camp in Pretoria. On stage was a group of native singers, musicians, and dancers from Soweto, politically the most seething black township in South Africa.

The incongruity of this moment shattered all the trappings and preconceptions so often attached to my limited, nearsighted view of Christianity. Here was a group of native South Africans dressed up in traditional Zulu costumes, playing a bizarre amalgamation of American rock and roll with tribal rhythms while they danced Zulu war dances and sang songs of praise in English in rich native harmonies to Jesus Christ the Lord on a summer evening in December.

There was only one common strain that wound around the stage and out through the racially and nationally mixed audience: we were all human beings in love with the same God and thankful for the love and hope that we were sharing together at that moment—a love and hope that we knew would eventually conquer all the divisions, barriers, hurts, and pains that seemed so inseparable from our earthly existence. But so much for the future; we were experiencing the future at that moment!

Realizing this, there was only one thing left for us to do, one thing that was appropriate for this celebration and common to us all. It happened without a word. Staid traditionalist and young rebel, black and white, Arminian and Calvinist, radical South African and National Security Force officer, Afrikaner and Zulu, Christian and non-Christian, all pushed back the chairs, cleared the floor, let the music play . . . and danced!

HIDE-AND-SEEK

*O*ne! ... Two! ... Three!...." Remember being *it* and pressing your forehead against the toad-skinned tree trunk, your body swaying impatiently back and forth while your dirty little fingers found loose bark to send prematurely to the ground? Remember hearing the scurrying in the yard and trying to memorize the location of the footsteps? And remember the urge to peek as you counted loudly . . . emphatically . . .

"Four! . . . Five! . . ."

Hide-and-seek is actually a very old game. The first man and woman on this planet hid from God—and they even made Him do the counting. How silly to hide from a God who sees everything. What a pointless game. But He played the game anyway and He continues to play with us—except that since that first game He's usually the One who hides. Once in a while we do get a glimpse of Him, but even when that happens, He always seems to beat us back to the tree. Then when we get our chance to hide, He always finds us. "How come I'm always the one who has to be *it*? . . . Six! . . . Seven! . . ."

That's exactly the attitude people have had throughout history in this cosmic game of hide-and-seek. In fact, they've often tried to stop the game by making images of God and announcing that they'd found Him, when all along the only thing they had was their own warped idea of what He was like.

Looking back, we also see that the game is hardly fair. Just think of all the places God has had to hide. There was the pillar of cloud by day and pillar of fire by night. There was the smoky fire at the peak of Mount Sinai, then the little golden box with wings on it. He hid in there for some time until they lost the box, and then He hid in the words and cries of prophets.

Finally, He fooled everyone and hid in a human body. Having donned this disguise, He acted on the strategy of speaking the truth in strange stories, answering questions with questions, and taking on the form of a lowly servant. They heard His voice, they saw Him do things only God could do, they looked Him right in the eye—but they still didn't find Him.

And when they'd had enough of the game, they crucified Him; they pounded nails through His hands and feet. He wouldn't hide from them again. Then, just in case, they sealed His dead body in a tomb. There. Game over. That would do it. No more hide-and-seek. But He made His greatest move of all.

He rose from the dead, broke out of the tomb, and so the game is still on!

"Eight! . . ."

That's the important thing. *Finding Him never means that the game is over.* It's impossible to have God within our grasp, for He cannot be fully understood, described, outlined, appreciated, measured, categorized, or wrapped up. So the game continues even after we think we've found Him—and, unfortunately, we're still *it.*

"Nine! . . ."

But that's all a part of the fun and the frustration of the game. The dirty palms, the fast breathing, the heart pounding so loudly we fear that it will give us away . . .

"Nine and a half! . . ."

There will always be those who, like the idolaters of old, try to create an image of God they can call on whenever they need something like a heaven-bound errand boy, someone to whom their dubious requests can be tossed. Maybe He becomes the president of their fan club: the ultimate ombudsman. He might be merely the greatest person they know—or know of—but He won't be God.

And there will always be writers of sermons and songs who tell us that God has been found and that we can go here or there to get whatever we need. But instead of finding God, they actually do away with Him. Reducing the Infinite, the Omniscient, and the Omnipotent to something we finite creatures can easily comprehend divests Him of His very nature. As soon as God is contained in a pat definition, He is easy to dismiss.

A wise old hide-and-seeker once said, "It is the glory of God to conceal a matter; to search out a matter is the glory of kings" (Prov. 25:2). Writers of sermons and songs who claim to tell everything there is to know about God are actually taking away His glory. They're also robbing their audience of the chance to seek—and robbing people of the search is robbing them of their chance to be kings.

Besides, seeking and finding, hiding and being found are all part of the challenge for those who are truly in the game.

"Nine and three quarters! . . . Ten! Ready or not, here I come!"

THE LORD OF THE DANCE

I danced in the morning when the world was begun,
And I danced in the moon and the stars and the sun.
I came down from heaven and I danced on the earth,
At Bethlehem I had my birth.

I danced for the scribe and the Pharisee,
But they would not dance and they wouldn't follow me.
I danced for the fishermen, for James and John,
They came with me and the dance went on.

Dance, dance, wherever you may be!
I am the Lord of the dance—said he—
And I'll lead you all wherever you may be,
And I'll lead you all in the dance—said he.

I danced on the Sabbath and I cured the lame.
The holy people said it was a shame.
They whipped and they stripped and they hung me high;
They left me there on a cross to die.

I danced on a Friday when the sky turned black.
It's hard to dance with the devil on your back.
They buried my body and they thought I'd gone,
But I am the dance and I still go on!

Dance, dance, wherever you may be!
I am the Lord of the dance—said he—
And I'll lead you all wherever you may be,
And I'll lead you all in the dance—said he.

They cut me down, but I leapt up high.
I am the life that will never, never die.
I'll live in you if you live in me,
I am the Lord of the dance—said he.

Dance, dance, wherever you may be!
I am the Lord of the dance—said he—
And I'll lead you all wherever you may be,
And I'll lead you all in the dance—said he.

—Sydney Carter

THE SPEAKER

*I*t was the eleventh hour. Aware of the power of the message and the critical nature of the hour, I mounted the platform. Adrenalin had kept me awake most of the night and the morning coffee had me buzzing, but I was ready to speak; not because I had been touched by God in some lofty place and had come down with words on stone, but because I had been scared out of my wits by the humble place I was forced to come to in order to hear God's message.

It was a critical hour for the people I was addressing, a critical hour for their country. But the Word of God which I shared had two edges: one for that moment, one for the future; one for the people, one for the preacher—and I felt the edge pointing at me then. I was feeling it hard against my chest. That was a critical hour for me as well.

"What did you go out into the desert to see?" I read Christ's words about John the Baptist from Matthew 11. "A reed swayed by the wind? If not, what did you go out to see? A man dressed in fine clothes? No, those who wear fine clothes are in kings' palaces. Then what did you go out to see? A prophet? Yes, I tell you, and more than a prophet."

I was dramatizing the Word and feeling its effect on the audience. "What audacity! A crazy man in the wilderness wearing camel's hair and eating locusts and honey! And this man was preparing the way for the Christ, the Anointed, the Savior of the world?"

The obviously radical nature of these strange workings of God in history excited me. Too many times, my backbone had swayed like a reed in the wind. Too many times I had felt uncomfortable in the fine clothes of a king. No more. I was determined to no longer compromise the Gospel, to no longer be patronized by men who claim it falsely.

I read on expressively: "From the days of John the Baptist until now, the kingdom of heaven has been forcefully advancing and forceful men lay hold of it." The Word had challenged me. For years I had been preaching a passive Gospel. Now, at a crucial time, God had led me to an aggressive laying hold of the kingdom of God. As I called the people to an aggressive love that would break down the racial religious, social, and political barriers in their divided country, I heard the call in my own ears: a call to love my wife.

I had also heard it, oddly enough, in the movie during my transAtlantic flight. "Define 'love,' " Starman had said. "Love is caring for someone more than you care for yourself," Jenny had replied. Her response had cut me to the quick. I had preached this theme countless times, but suddenly, in the context of a science fiction movie, I had understood it as if for the first time. I had never let anyone else steal time from my own concerns— as my wife's present emotional state and the situation at home evidenced. Nourishing and cherishing her as God commanded would mean laying hold of the kingdom of God.

I read on. "To what can I compare this generation? They are like children sitting in the marketplaces and calling out to others, 'We played the flute for you, and you did not dance; we sang a dirge, and you did not mourn.' "

"They were asleep," I told my audience. "They were dulled by their own complacency, their ease, their noninvolvement in life. They never laid hold of anything. The sorrow wasn't there and the joy wasn't there. The dance of life was left for children, not for adults who knew better.

187

"You must attach yourself to the pain that divides this country. You can't ignore it and hope that it will go away. You must mourn over it, but you can also bind yourself to the love that can unite this country. You can discover that you are your country's hope. You can do something about the problems; and in doing something, you can dance the dance of life."

I finished my message just as Christ finished His. " 'Wisdom is proved right by her actions'—and this is a time for action," I concluded, "a time for radical Christianity, and a time for Christians to aggressively support the dignity of the individual regardless of race, and to model an overcoming love that breaks down walls to the world."

As I sat down, I was not thinking about the impact of my message, the significance of my trip, the reasons why I almost had not come, nor of the now-clear evidence why God sent me. Instead, I was aware of the things in my own life that I could no longer ignore, things I had hoped would go away. Like each one of us, I had to act—and in doing what I had to do, I have freed myself to dance.

ROUND ABOUT

I stood at the side of the stage and stared up through the scaffold into the blue sky. Grabbing the bars, I pulled and stretched my body to make more room in my lungs for air.

Normally this was an anxious moment. The few minutes that precede a concert are notoriously plagued by scattered attention and last-minute panics. This time was different. There was a groundswell of confidence, a sense of inevitable success that everyone—even the audience—seemed to feel.

For once I wanted to hold this moment, to savor the strength. I noticed everything I could and recorded it in my mind. I listened to the random notes of the band tuning up, heard the final instructions for the stage crew, and caught eye-glance encouragement from the stage manager. I could see that many in the crowd were standing . . . waiting. Why? They had never stood and waited this way for me before. Somehow they knew too.

"How's that sound to you?" the monitor mixer questioned me about my guitar equalization. "A little more on the high end, please," I replied, more out of amusement than out of necessity. I could play my guitar today even if it sounded like a banjo through a broken speaker. There was enough power and purpose in my heart to do this concert if everything went wrong, yet enough confidence to know that nothing would.

Returning to the scaffold, I threw back my head once again and stared into the sky as if to drink in wholeness from my Creator. Every fiber of my being seemed to know: *this* was what I was made for. A smile that just would not go away formed on my face.

Suddenly it seemed to me that I had lived my life backwards. Once I had been old, knowing all the answers. I had even known the answers before the questions were asked—like the game show contestant punching the button before the host could even complete the question. Now I realized that I must have punched the button on lots of people, and I felt a twinge of remorse. I had thought myself wise first, instead of last. As a young man, I had held back, not wanting to lay out my pearls before swine. I had been a wise old kid, thinking that wisdom could somehow precede experience.

Now I felt young, reckless, energetic—anxious to live a life that I had only commented on for so long. I felt cheated out of youth, but I was determined not to let my life pass without enjoying its full expression. The answers, however true, had only served to trap me inside my quiet, theoretical self. I had finally become aware of something more important than being right: it was called being awake, being alive, being in touch with my heart, with my spirit, and with humanity. Now I would rather be wrong and know this than be right and be a stone.

As I watched a wisp of cloud pass over the scaffold, I knew I had found both—I was awake *and* I was right.

Suddenly my guitar was plugged in and on my shoulder. I was introduced and the crowd was up. From the first chord to the last, the power of love and truth shot from my heart to the people—from heart to heart—I knew I'd made the connection.

For years I had been a Christian, but I had not always known what that meant. The pain of reaching out, the risk of growing, the open gashes of truth had finally culminated in this moment.

For so long my Christianity had touched my head and delivered the answers like dinner on a plate. Now it had touched my heart: the music had become one with me, and what I shared that day was not a message—though there was one—or mere lists of answers—though there were many. What I shared in that moment with five thousand people was the essence of a man seeking after God, truth, and wholeness. The music was in me and I was in the music. I knew now that this was all that was to be expected from me—no more and, most certainly, no less.

As I sang, my eyes were filled with wonder, with tears, with stinging sweat, with other eyes, with joy, and with laughter. For even though I had known this was going to happen, I couldn't possibly have known that it was going to be as wonderful as this. And as I connected with my music, I also connected with 5,000 people who simply couldn't stand still.

What do you know! Real Christians do dance . . . after all!